Legal information

© 2022
Author and Editor: M.Eng. Johannes Wild
A94689H39927F
Email: 3dtech@gmx.de
Web: www.3dtech-3dprinting.com
The complete imprint of the book can be found on the last pages!

This work is protected by copyright

Thank you so much for choosing this book!

Foreword

Thank you very much for choosing this book!

If you are looking for a practical guide for the easy to learn, yet very versatile programming language Python, then you are in the right place and well advised with this book! I am an engineer (M.Eng.) and would like to introduce you to the world of programming with Python simply explained. You will learn in this book both the theoretical basics of programming in Python, as well as the practical application using a lot of examples and also DIY projects. This book offers you an easy-to-understand, intuitively structured and practical introduction to the world of programming with Python! No matter whether Python 2 or Python 3!

This fundamentals book is specifically for anyone who has no or very primitive prior knowledge of programming and Python, but also for anyone who wants to learn Python as another programming language. No matter what age you are, what profession you have, whether you are a pupil, student or pensioner. This book is for anyone who wants (or needs) to learn about the fascinating subject of programming.

The goal of this book is to teach you step by step what the basics in Python are and how to successfully apply them to program your own scripts. So in this Python basic course you will learn everything you need to know as a beginner! The best thing to do is take a look inside the book and get your copy as an e-book or paperback!

The book is structured as intuitively as possible. This means that, especially in the first examples, there may well be code fragments that you will not yet understand, as these will be explained in detail later. If this is the case, please do not let this irritate you, but simply continue and always focus only on the part of the example code that has just been explained or has already been explained. As the reading progresses, you will then understand more and more of the program code of the examples in the learning process. Be sure to stick with it, even if it gets a little more complicated! Python is worth it!

Table of Contents

Foreword 2

Table of Contents...3

1 Why Python?..6

2 Setting up the Python environment on Windows.................................8

3 Introduction to Python..13

4 Python syntax 17

4.1 Implicit line continuation 18

4.2 Explicit line continuation..19

4.3 Comments in Python..19

4.4 Spaces in Python 21

5 Variables, arrays, strings and tuples...23

5.1 Variables..23

5.2 Arrays 27

5.2.1 Create Python arrays 28

5.2.2 Adding elements to an array... 30

5.2.3 Access to elements of an array 32

5.2.4 Removing elements from the array 32

5.2.5 Division of an array 32

5.2.6 Search element in an array 34

5.2.7 Updating elements in an array.. 34

5.3 Strings (character string or string of characters).............................35

5.3.1 Creation of a string 36

5.3.2 Accessing characters in a string 38

5.3.3 Slicing of strings (character strings) 39

5.3.4 Deleting / updating strings 40

5.3.5 Escape characters in a string... 42

5.3.6 Special string operators 43

5.3.7 Special operator for formatting strings...................................... 44

5.3.8 Arithmetic operators 45

5.4 Tuple 46

5.4.1 Concatenation of tuples 47

5.4.2 Nesting of tuples 48

5.4.3 Repetitions in tuples 48

5.4.4 Invariability of tuples 49

5.4.5 Division of tuples 49

5.4.6 Deleting elements in a tuple 50

5.4.7 Predefined functions for tuples 51

6 Functions 53

6.1 Defining a Function 53

6.2 Docstring 54

6.3 The return statement 55

6.4 Calling a function 56

6.5 Arguments of a Function 56

6.6 Pass by reference 61

7 Loops and Conditions 63

7.1 Loops 63

7.1.1 While loop 63

7.1.2 For loop 64

7.2 Conditions 64

7.2.1 If statement 64

7.2.2 else statement 65

7.2.3 elif statement 66

7.2.4 Nested if statement 67

7.2.5 The short-hand statements for if and else 68

7.2.6 Logical operators 69

8 Other important basics in Python 71

8.1 Possibility to enter a text by a user 71

8.2 Insert current date & time in Python 71

8.3 The try-except statement and its use 72

9 Basics of object-oriented programming (OOP) 73

9.1 Classes 74

9.2 The definition of a class 75

9.3 Objects of a class 75

9.4 Declaring / Instantiating objects 75

9.5 The "__init__" method 76

10 GUI Development with Python 78

10.1 The Tkinter GUI development package/library 79

10.2 Tkinter widgets 80

10.2.1 Button 80

10.2.2 Canvas (graphic area) 82

10.2.3 Check button widget (selection button) 86

10.2.4 Entry widget (entry-widget) 88

10.2.5 Frame widget (Frame widget) 90

10.2.6 Label widget 91

11 DIY projects 93

11.1 Project 1: A simple calculator with user input 93

11.2 Project 2: Display of all prime numbers in an interval 97

11.3 Project 3: Calculator with graphical user interface (GUI) 100

12 Troubleshooting - common beginner mistakes 115

Closing words 116

1 Why Python?

Before we start with the basics of programming, in this first chapter we will take a look at why our decision to use Python was right and whether it is worth learning a programming language. Python is one of the most popular programming languages of our time. Why ? On the one hand, because Python is very user-friendly and very easy to learn, and on the other hand, because the Python programming language has a wide range of functions that can be used not only for simple use cases, but also for complex ones. Let's take a look at a few more aspects and advantages of Python, so that we can make sure that Python brings us the best start in programming.

Open Source

Python is an open-source programming language that thrives and grows on community support and contributions. The term open source is generally characterized by the fact that the software is freely available, active user participation is desired, and there are no restrictions on use. You can download the official Python software IDLE ("Interactive Development Environment") for free from the Python website. We will look at how this works in detail in a moment.

Availability of Libraries

Python has a very large number of additional libraries. What are libraries? A library represents an extension that allows us to quickly and easily implement additional functions or code. It is basically nothing more than code that has already been written by developers in the community. Most libraries can be found on platforms like GitHub (github.com) or Stackoverflow (stackoverflow.com). These websites are a kind of administrative platform / developer community for software development. If there are many libraries to choose from, this has the great advantage that beginners or even advanced users do not have to develop every single function from scratch. Since some (e.g. basic) functions are needed again and again and this also usually by other users, often someone already took care of the development of the code for a function and made this available. By already developed packages and modules one can use and/or implement this function then directly. Thus one can concentrate on the actual code and/or the actual function of a program. In a figurative sense, you could compare this to a car ride. You can get directly into a car and use components such as steering wheel, accelerator pedal, or air conditioning for the actual journey and do not have to construct the car for it or create individual functions.

Readability

Python can be read very well - even by beginners. This programming language is not quite as abstract as some others, where a beginner trying to read the programming language does not understand anything at first. This means even a beginner can easily understand the functionality of the Python program to some extent. This is also helped by the fact that Python uses simple indentations for separation instead of semicolons (which is the case with other programming languages like C, for example), which makes the Python program code look very structured compared to other programming languages.

Object-oriented and functional programming

Python supports object-oriented programming. We will look at what object-oriented programming is in detail in a later chapter. For now, let's just say that object-oriented programming reduces the complexity of larger programs and makes them much easier to work with.

However, Python not only supports object-oriented programming, but functional programming can also be used, which is built on the use of functions. We will also look at functions in a later chapter.

Platform-independent

The final argument in favor of learning Python is that it is a platform-independent programming language, which means that the developer can write a Python program in any interactive development environment and run it on different operating systems such as Microsoft Windows, Mac, or Linux.

In the next chapter we will first set up the Python environment and then start programming in the chapter after next. Let's go!

2 Setting up the Python environment on Windows

In Windows, the Python development environment is not included by default. Therefore we have to install this so-called **IDLE** first. With Mac or Linux, Python is already pre-installed from certain versions and can be used immediately. With Linux, for example, it is sufficient to enter the command Python3 in the Linux terminal to open it. However, setting up the Python programming environment on Windows is also very simple and is explained step by step below. It is recommended to use the official Python development environment IDLE (Interactive Development Environment).

Step 1: Download Python executable installer

Download the desired version, preferably the latest version, of the Python installer from the official Python website:

https://www.python.org/downloads/windows

Select the correct "Windows Installer" file in the "Stable Releases" section.

Here you need to distinguish whether you have a 32-bit version of Windows or a 64-bit version of Windows installed on your PC. If you don't know this, right-click in the "This PC" folder on your PC and click on "Properties". The system type will then be displayed. If in doubt, simply start with the 64-bit version. If this cannot be installed correctly because you have a 32-bit version of Windows, an error message will be displayed anyway.

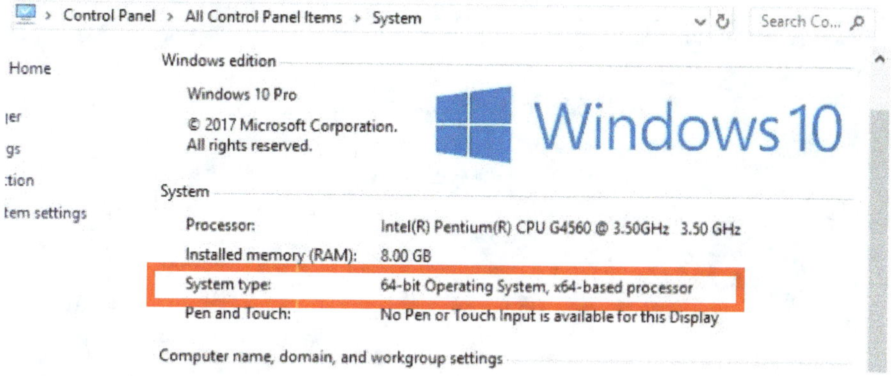

Step 2: Launch the installation program

Launch the Python installer once the download process is complete.

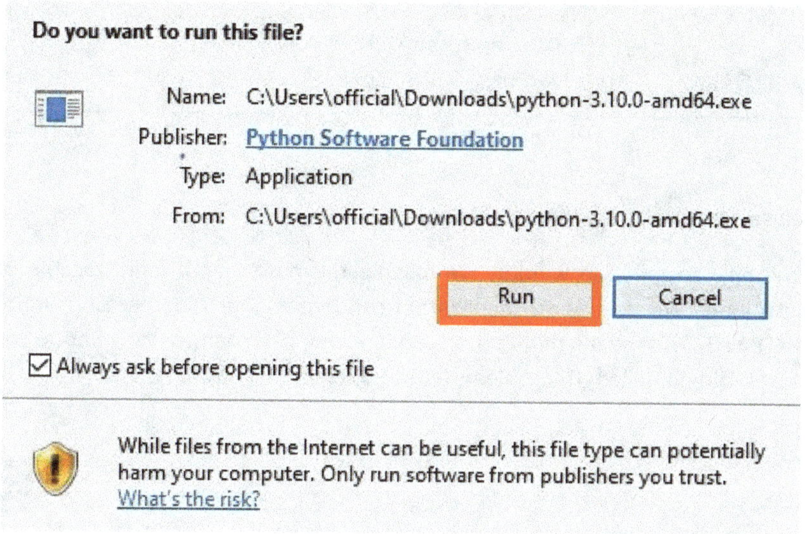

Then check the following options in the installation window at the bottom:

1) Install launcher for all users (recommended)

2) Add Python ... to PATH

For all newer versions of Python, the recommended **PIP** and **IDLE** installation options are already included. Older versions may not include these additional features.

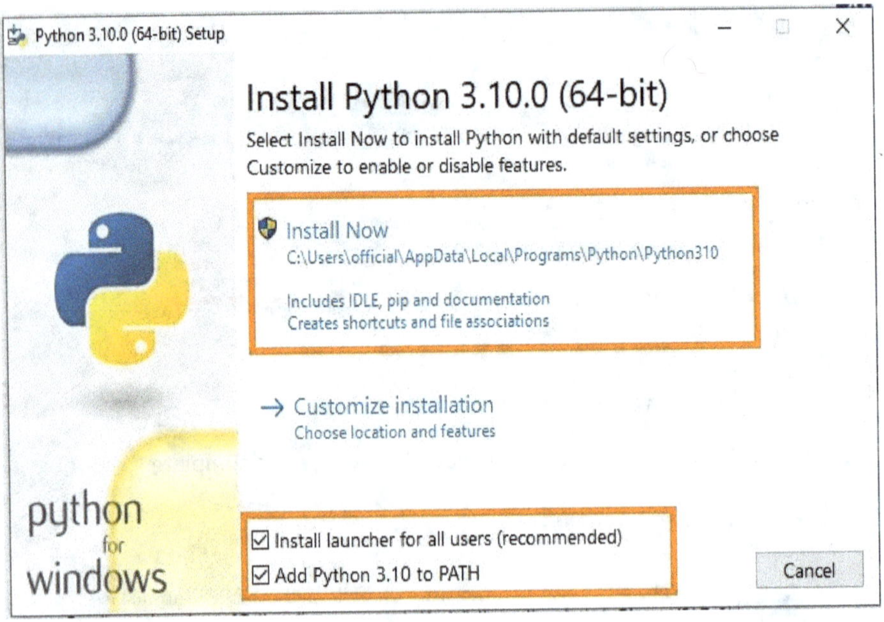

Then select **Install now** for installation.

In the next installation window we **disable** the path length limit: **disable path length limit**. We do this so that Python can bypass the 260 character limit for **MAX_PATH.** This means that Python can use long path names. We need to select this to avoid name length problems later. So select this option.

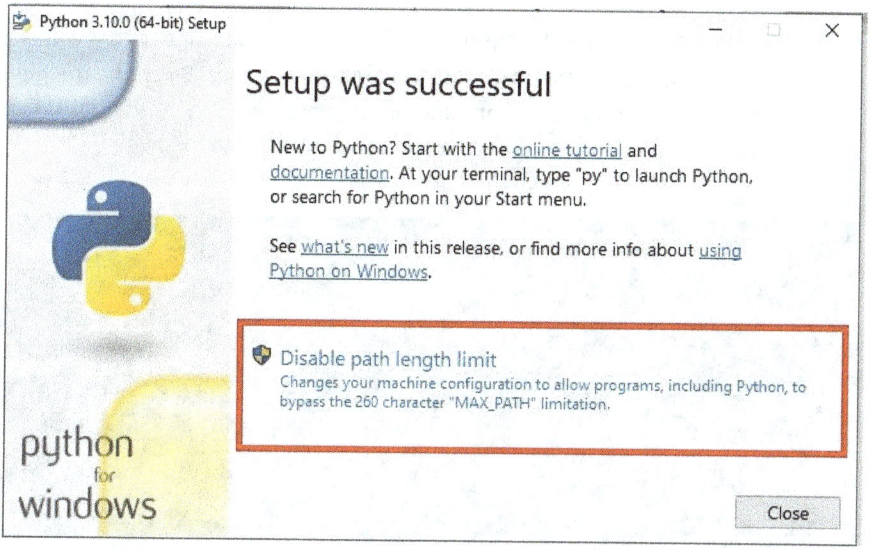

Step 3: Check if the installation was successful and if PIP is available

To check if the installation was successful, we open the **command** prompt in Windows. You can simply search for this using the term **cmd** in the Windows taskbar search function and open it. We enter the command **python -V** in the command prompt and press Enter.

If the installation was successful, your installed version of Python should then be displayed here. In our case it is **Python 3.10.0**.

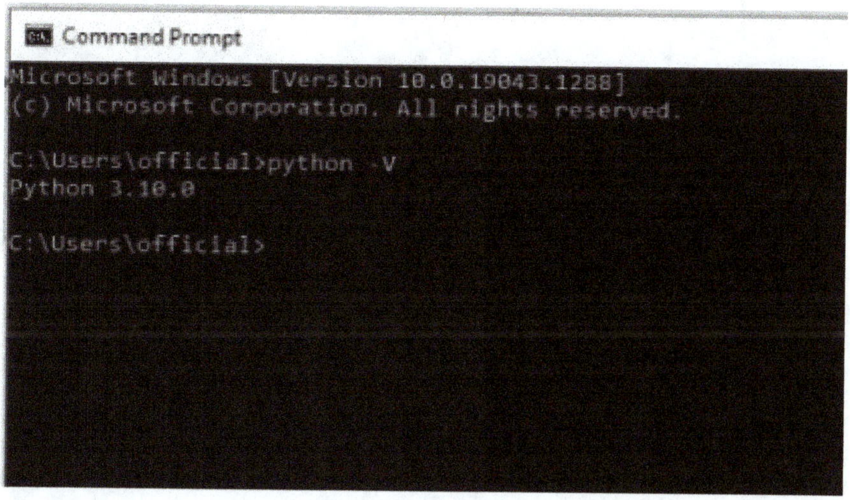

Then we check if **PIP** is available. **PIP** stands for **pip installs packages** and is a useful management system for Python libraries and Python packages. By typing the **pip -V** command at the command prompt and hitting Enter, we can verify that it was successfully installed. You should see something similar to the following:

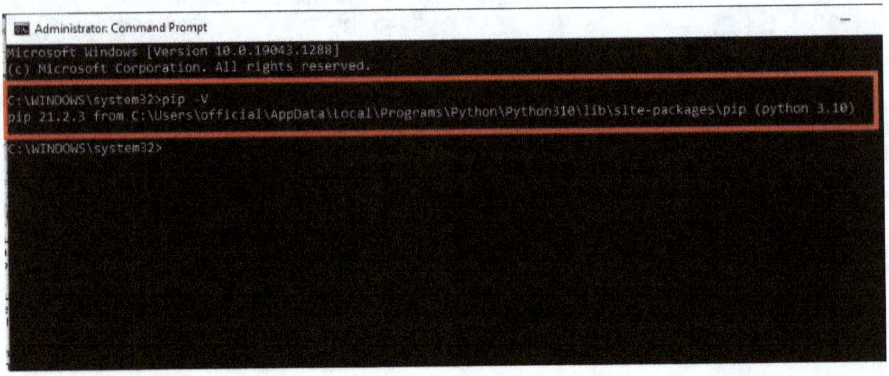

In the next lesson we will get an overview of the Python IDLE, i.e. the development environment. After that we will get to the Python syntax and the first programming attempts.

3 Introduction to Python

Now we have installed everything necessary and finally come to the Python IDLE (Interactive Development Environment), i.e. the software environment. In the further course we will deal with the Python syntax and the first programming examples. Syntax is the term for the rules for the use of characters in a programming language and the structural design of the code.

By the way: The last lesson contains a troubleshooting guide, which can help you with debugging, if a script does not work. Take a look at this lesson as soon as the first errors occur.

An overview of the Python IDLE:

The Python IDLE is a relatively slim program, which actually consists only of an input window (text editor) and a menu bar, in the upper area. To open the Pyhton-IDLE, simply search for the term IDLE in the search function of the taskbar. The following window should then open:

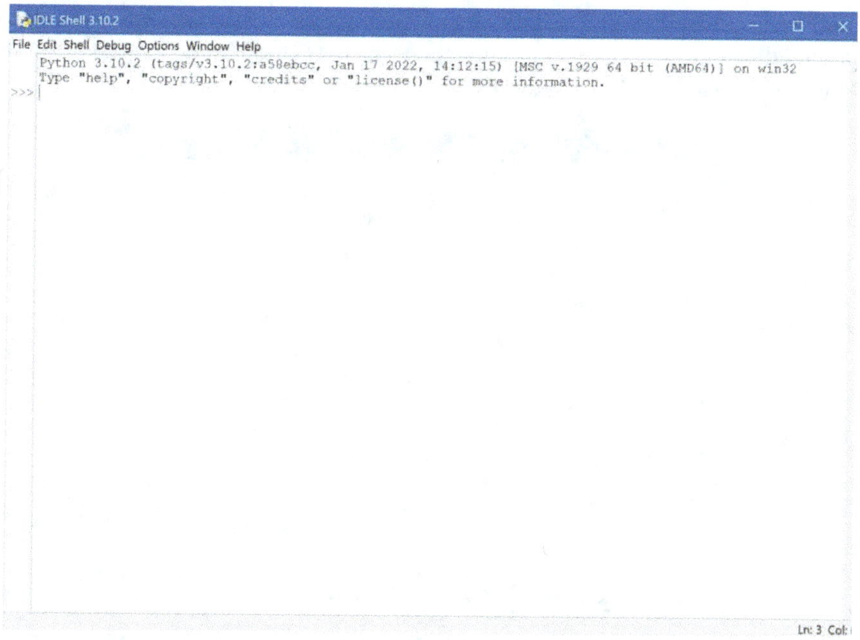

We will briefly discuss some important functions of the menu bar below and then move on to Python syntax. In the menu bar in the File tab you will find basic functions like creating a new file or opening and of course saving a file. To begin, click **New File** here and then save the newly opened window under a desired name.

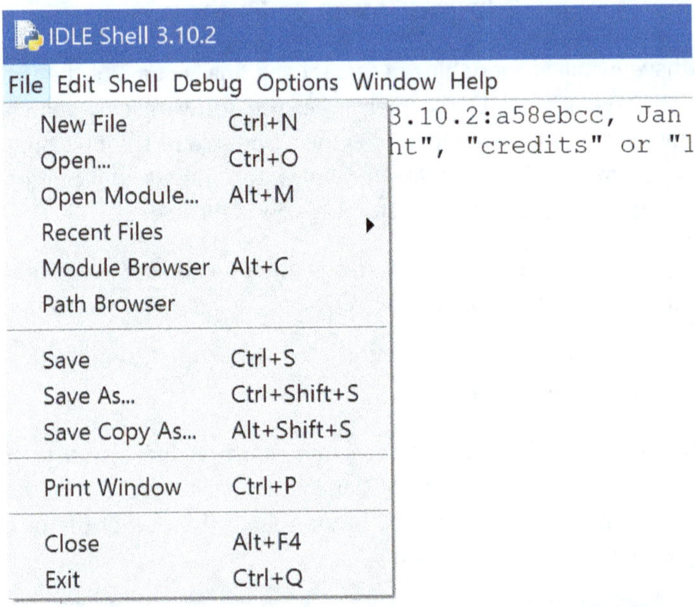

In the **Edit** menu tab you will find functions such as Undo, Redo or Paste or Cut. However, these are self-explanatory.

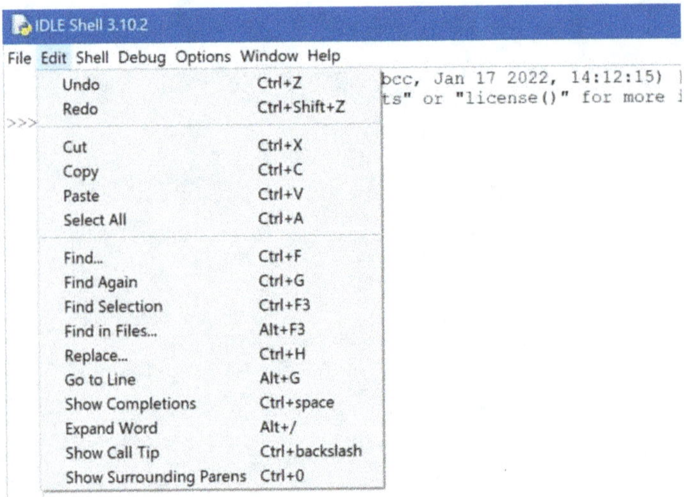

If you now open a new script under **File**, you will find a slightly modified menu bar that also contains the important **Format** and **Run** tabs. In **Format** you can, for example, specify indentations and comments, but we will learn what these are and how to do them in a moment.

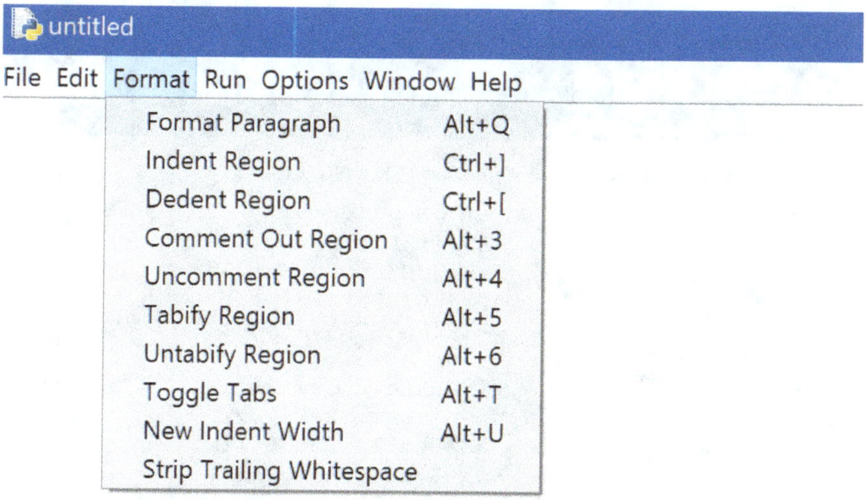

When you have finished the code for a program that you write directly into the input window, you can start the execution of the script in the **Run** tab (be sure to save it beforehand) or even check the module first.

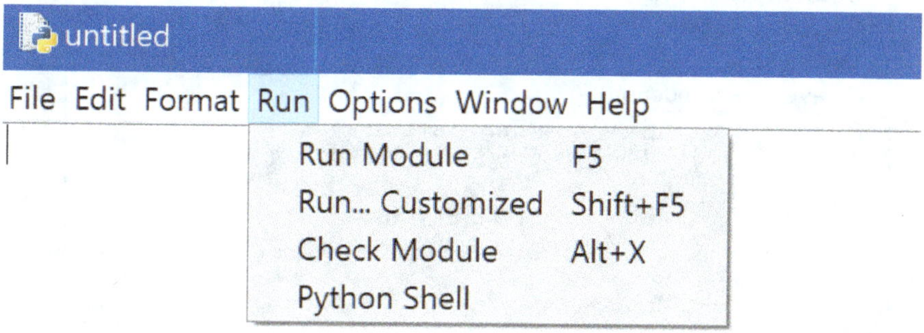

Finally, you can use the **Options** tab to configure the IDLE according to your individual preferences. Here you can set different fonts or colors, for example. The other two tabs (**Window** and **Help**) are rather unimportant and self-explanatory.

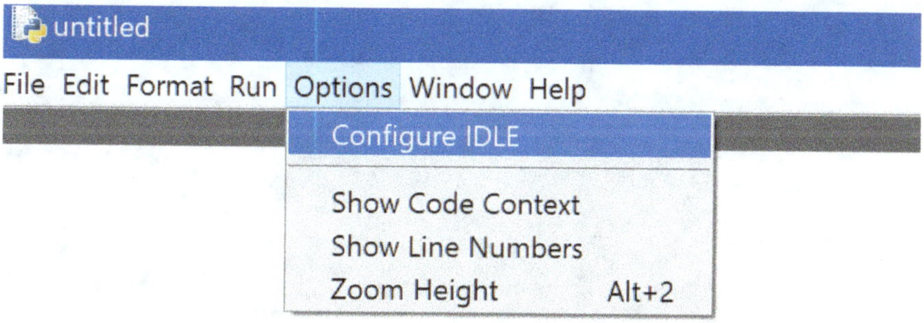

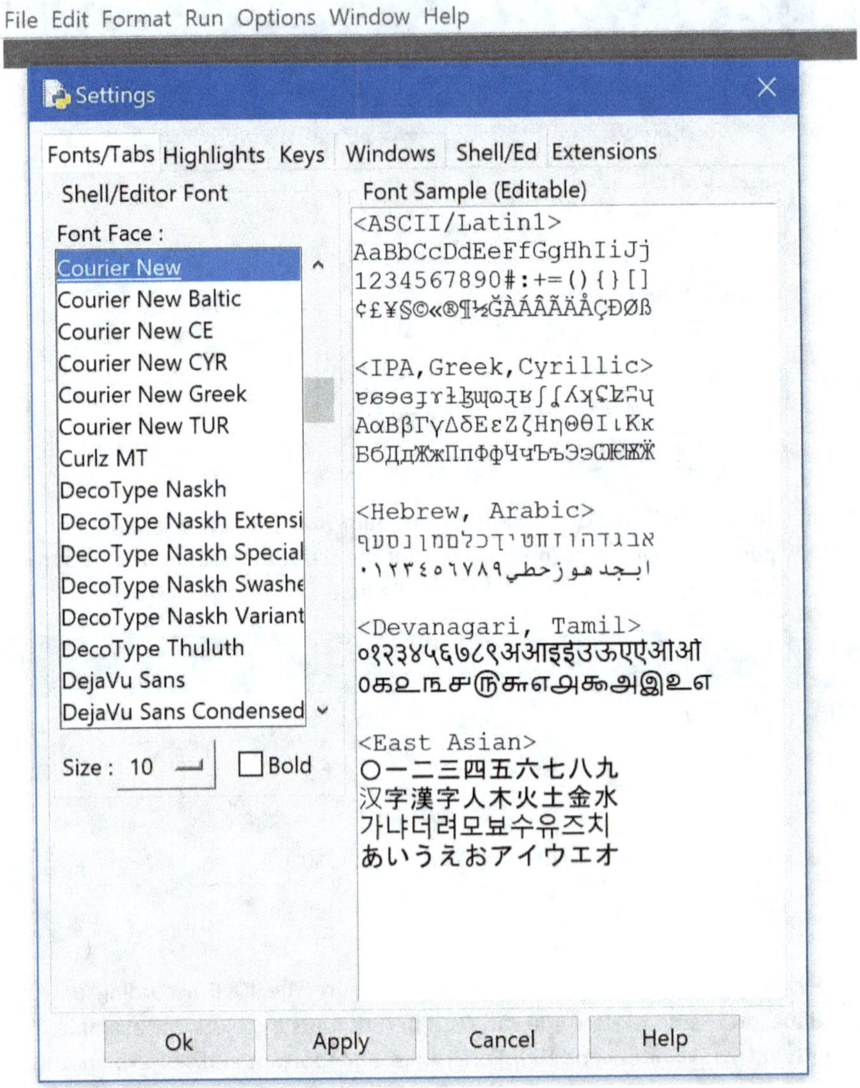

File Edit Format Run Options Window Help
Settings
Fonts/Tabs
Highlights
Keys
Windows
Shell/Ed
Extensions
Shell/Editor Font
Font Face :
Courier New
Courier New Baltic
Courier New CE
Courier New CYR
Courier New Greek
Courier New TUR
Curlz MT
DecoType Naskh
DecoType Naskh Extensi
DecoType Naskh Special
DecoType Naskh Swashe
DecoType Naskh Variant
DecoType Thuluth
DejaVu Sans
DejaVu Sans Condensed
Size : 10
Bold
Font Sample (Editable)
<ASCII/Latin1>
AaBbCcDdEeFfGgHhIiJj
1234567890#:+=(){}[]
<IPA,Greek,Cyrillic>
<Hebrew, Arabic>
<Devanagari, Tamil>
<East Asian>
〇一二三四五六七八九
汉字漢字人木火土金水
가냐더려모뵤수유즈치
あいうえおアイウエオ
Ok
Apply
Cancel
Help

4 Python syntax

A program code is written in Python in such a way that each instruction is on a separate line. This is because, normally, Python reads the statements line by line and then executes them (sequential execution). However, there are cases where the flow may deviate from this line-by-line reading and execution. So, normally, Python statements are written so that there is only one statement per line.

However, it is also possible to write several statements in a single line. Then one uses a semicolon for the separation between these instructions. However, for an orderly structure, as well as for good readability of the code, it is recommended to write only one statement per line, especially if it is not very simple or longer. By the way, the term **print(...)** in the following examples is a function that, as the name suggests, simply prints the content that is in the parentheses after it (text must be in quotes). But what functions are, how to use them, and how to create your own, we will learn in detail later. And by the way, from here on, it's best to just program all the examples yourself, that way you'll learn most effectively!

Example a):

File Edit Format Run Options Window Help

```
print("Welcome to Python")
```

Output a):

```
Welcome to Python
```

Example b):

File Edit Format Run Options Window Help

```
a = 50; b = 100; c = a + b

print(a); print(b); print(c)
```

Output b):

```
50
100
150
```

If a statement in a line is so long that it no longer fits on the screen, you would have to scroll back and forth. To avoid this, you can use line continuation. This allows you to write a single statement in multiple lines to increase readability. Line continuation can be divided into two types depending on how it is implemented: a) implicit line continuation and b) explicit line continuation.

4.1 Implicit line continuation

This type can be seen as the simpler form of line continuation. Implicit continuation means that any statement containing open round brackets, i.e. **(**, open square brackets **[**, or open curly brackets **{**, remains incomplete until the corresponding closing bracket is set. In this way, the same statement can be continued over several lines or even longer without an error occurring.

Example a):

File Edit Format Run Options Window Help

```
a = [
    [1, 2, 3],
    [4, 5, 6],
    [7, 8, 9]
    ]

print(a)
```

Output a):

```
[[1, 2, 3], [4, 5, 6], [7, 8, 9]]
```

Example b):

File Edit Format Run Options Window Help

```
subject_1 = int(input("Enter subject_1 marks: "))
subject_2 = int(input("Enter subject_2 marks: "))
subject_3 = int(input("Enter subject_3 marks: "))
subject_4 = int(input("Enter subject_4 marks: "))

if (
    subject_1 >= 45 and
    subject_2 >= 50 and
    subject_3 >= 48 and
    subject_4 >= 50
    ):

    print("This student successfully completed the semester.")

else:
    print("The required marks have not been obtained to pass the semester.")
```

Output b):

```
Enter subject_1 marks: 68
Enter subject_2 marks: 74
Enter subject_3 marks: 81
Enter subject_4 marks: 78
This student successfully completed the semester.
```

4.2 Explicit line continuation

This type of line continuation is used in cases where the previously learned implicit continuation is not applicable. In this method, a backslash is used to make the Python interpreter understand that the respective line is also continued in the next line. The backslash must be the last character of the line to be continued.

Example a):

File Edit Format Run Options Window Help

```
a = \
    5 + 8 \
    + 10 + 7 \
    + 20

print (a)
```

Output a):

```
50
>>>
```

4.3 Comments in Python

In order for yourself and another programmer to better understand more complex code and to better follow the flow of a code, you can set comments in Python. These are simply hints that do not affect the code and are simply ignored by the Python interpreter. Thus, comments are only for human understanding. Comments increase the readability and comprehensibility of the script and contribute to debugging. To make the Python interpreter understand that a text is a comment, you can proceed in two ways: a) write line-by-line comments or b) write section-by-section comments.

Line-by-line comments:

Line-by-line comments are marked in a Python script with the hash symbol **#**, which must be placed at the beginning of the text or comment. If the hash symbol is inside a line or text, it does not become a comment.

Example a):

```
#This is a single line comment
```

Example b):

```
a = 'This is # not a comment #'
print(a) # Prints the string stored in variable a
```

Section-by-Section Comments:

Paragraph comments are annotations written across multiple lines. These are started or ended in Python by three consecutive quotation marks """. That is, three quotes are placed at the beginning of the section that is to be considered a comment, then the comment follows as text, and three more quotes are placed at the end of the text.

Example a):

```
""" This is a
multiple line
comment
"""
```

Example b):

```
""" The following statement prints the string stored
    in the variable "a" """

a = 'This is # not a comment #'
print(a) # Prints the string stored in variable a
```

4.4 Spaces in Python

Spaces are usually ignored in Python (exceptions follow) and are not taken into account by the Python interpreter, but it is still advantageous to avoid unnecessary spaces from the start.

First exception: If, for example, you need to separate an element from variables or other keywords, spaces are even required.

Example a):

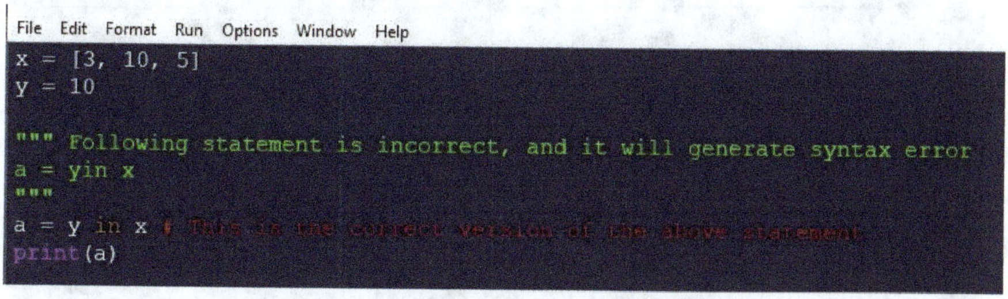
File Edit Format Run Options Window Help
x = [3, 10, 5]
y = 10
""" Following statement is incorrect, and it will generate syntax error
a = yin x
"""
a = y in x # This is the correct version of the above statement
print(a)

Second exception: Spaces can also be used as indentations.

Indentation simply means that the text starts a little further to the right. This serves to structure a program code. Therefore, you should not insert unnecessary spaces in the middle or at the beginning of the script, so that they are not considered indentations. This can change the functionality of the script or result in an error.

Example b):

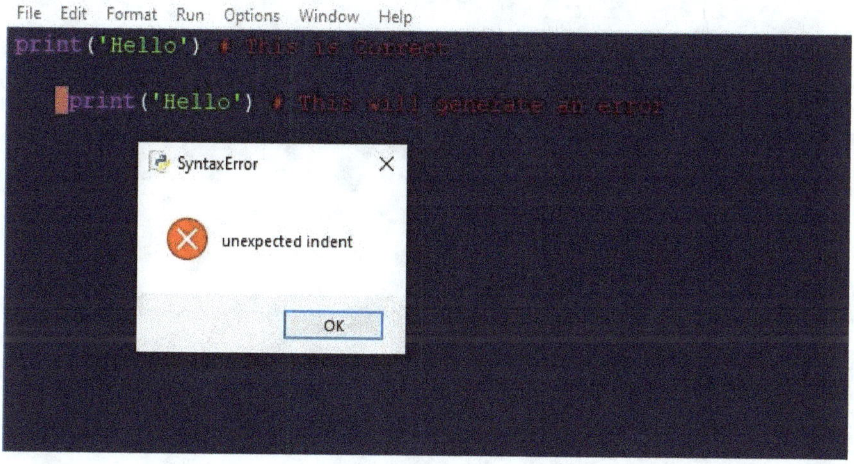

So why do you need these indentations at all? You create indentations to determine the grouping of statements like loops or control structures. These indentations are created, as already mentioned, by inserting spaces before a statement. Alternatively, you can use the menu bar or the tab key.

Example c):

File Edit Format Run Options Window Help

```
a = 10

while(a != 0):
    if(a > 5):      # line 1
        print('a > 5')   # line 2
    else:           # line 3
        print('a < 5')  # line 4
    a -= 2          # line 5

"""
Lines 1, 3, 5 are on same level
Line 2 will only be executed if if condition becomes true.
Line 4 will only be executed if if condition becomes false.
"""
```

5 Variables, arrays, strings and tuples

5.1 Variables

In simple terms, a variable can be used to define and store a value. Such a value can be, for example, a number or a character. A variable is therefore a data element that links a name or a letter with an assigned value. Defining a variable is called declaring a variable in the programming language.

Variables do not have to be explicitly declared with the data type in Python, i.e. you do not have to mention the type of the variable (**integer**, **string,** ...) in the declaration to be able to use it. In other programming languages, however, you do have to.

Rules for naming Python variables:

Below are a few rules of thumb to follow when using variable names in Python to avoid complications:

1) Variables can be started with either a letter (upper or lower case) or an underscore. The rest of the variable can then contain upper or lower case letters, underscores and also numbers. The value of the variable is assigned with an equal sign =.

Example a):

File Edit Format Run Options Window Help

```
ThisIsaValidVariable_07 = 10
print(ThisIsaValidVariable_07)
```

Output a):

```
10
>>>
```

2) Python variables are case sensitive because the Python language itself is case sensitive. So be sure to observe this in the Python script.

Example b):

File Edit Format Run Options Window Help

```
name = 'Python'
print(Name)
```

Output b):

```
NameError: name 'Name' is not defined
>>>
```

3) There are words that are already reserved by the Python interpreter. Such words cannot be used as variable names, otherwise there will be overlaps. These are, for example, the following:

and	def	False	import	not	True
as	del	finally	in	or	try
assert	elif	for	is	pass	while
break	else	from	lambda	print	with
class	except	global	None	raise	yield
continue	exec	if	nonlocal	return	

Example c):

File Edit Format Run Options Window Help

```
True = accept
```

Output c):

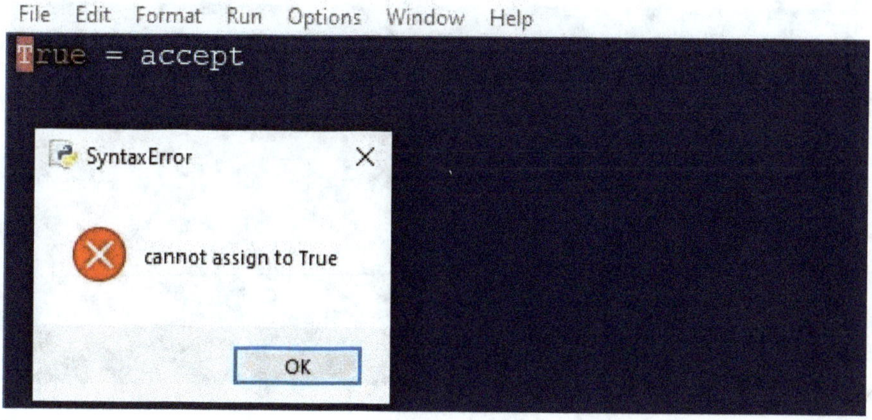

4) An equals sign = is used, as mentioned earlier, when assigning a value to a variable. The variable name should be on the left side of the equal sign and the variable value on the right side of the equal sign.

Example d):

File Edit Format Run Options Window Help

```
a = 5         # An integer assignment
b = 3.5       # A floating point
c = "total"   # A string
```

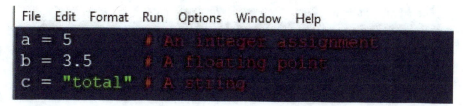

If, on the other hand, the name and value are reversed, as in the following example, an error occurs.

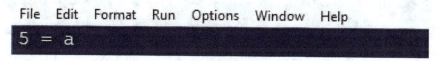

Example e):

File Edit Format Run Options Window Help

```
5 = a
```

Output (e):

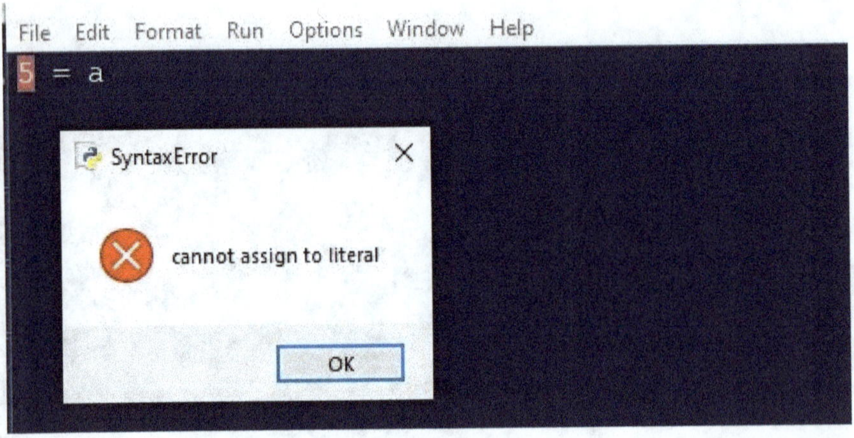

6) You can assign different values to several variables at the same time (but not different values to only one variable). To do this, use a comma to separate the variables or values.

Example f):

File Edit Format Run Options Window Help

```
name, age = 'john', 25
print(name, age)
```

Output f):

```
john 25
>>>
```

7) You can assign the same value to several variables at the same time. To do this, use a = character between the variables and the value.

Example g):

```
category=grade='A'
print(category,grade)
```

Output g):

```
A A
>>> |
```

8) You can delete variables in Python with the term **del.** After that this variable will not be recognized anymore.

Example h):

```
name = 'mark'
print(name)
del name
```

Output h):

```
Traceback (most recent call last):
  File "C:\Users\official\Documents\Python\4.py", line 4, in <module>
    print(name)
NameError: name 'name' is not defined
>>> |
```

5.2 Arrays

With the help of an array, several values can be stored one after the other in one element. Similar to a variable, but in a larger number. A specific stored value can then be addressed by the respective index. One can imagine it pictorially as follows: Let's assume that each passenger of a bus is assigned a seat (10 passengers and 10 seats) with a number. We could do this with the help of e.g. 10 single variables. But we can also do it in one step using an array. The single passenger with seat number would be a value in this case, the bus would be the array. All passengers sit down in the bus on their assigned seat number (who sits where is described by the index).

More abstractly, we can take a simplified look at this first in the following example, which is followed by Python-specific examples.

Variable: *x = 10*

y = 20

z = 30

...

Array:

array_bus = (10,20,30,40,50,60,70,80,90,100)

Caution: In Python the notation is then somewhat different, that follows shortly in another example. This notation is only for simplified explanation.

The elements here would be our seats with the passengers and the number of seats would be determined with the size (Size) of the array (in our case the bus).

Depending on which value you want to address (or which passenger of the bus) you use the respective index of the value in the array.

Index 0 of array_bus : assigned value = 10 (because it is the first value in the array)

Index 1 of array_bus: assigned value = 20 (because it is the second value in the array)

etc. ...

The use of arrays in Python makes it easier to access the individual elements through this simple indexing.

5.2.1 Create Python arrays

First you need to import the array module into the script with **import...as**:

```
# Creation of Python Array

# importing "array" module for array creation
import array as arr
```

Then arrays can be created with the function **array(argument 1, argument 2)**, where *argument 1* and *argument 2* specify the respective data type and values. For example, in the following we create an array of the data type **integer (i)** (= first argument) with the values: 10, 20, 30, 40, 50 (= second argument).

```
# Creation of Python Array

# importing "array" module for array operations
import array as arr

# creating an array with integer type
a = arr.array('i', [10, 20, 30, 40, 50])
```

Finally we can display the array and a text with **print():**

```
# Creation of Python Array

# importing "array" module for array operations
import array as arr

# creating an array with integer type
a = arr.array('i', [10, 20, 30, 40, 50])

# printing original array
print ("The new created Integer array is : ", end =" ")
for i in range (0, 5):
    print (a[i], end =" ")
print()
```

Output:

```
The new created Integer array is :  10 20 30 40 50
```

We need the **for** loop so that all values are displayed (**range** 0-5, i.e. index 0-5). But more about loops later!

For practice purposes, define an array of the data type **float** (**d**) with the following values: 1.5, 2.4, 3.6, 4.6, 5.4 and display it with **print().** The procedure is analogous and the solution follows immediately, so pause briefly and try it on your own.

Solution or input:

File Edit Format Run Options Window Help

```
# Creation of Python Array

# importing "array" module for array operations
import array as arr
```

```
# creating an array with float type
b = arr.array('d', [1.5, 2.4, 3.6, 4.6, 5.4])

# printing original array
print ("The new created Float array is : ", end =" ")
for i in range (0, 5):
    print (b[i], end =" ")
```

Output:

```
The new created Float array is :  1.5 2.4 3.6 4.6 5.4
>>> |
```

In the previous examples, the letters "**i**" and "**d**" determine the data type of the array when it is created. These are also referred to as type code.

5.2.2 Adding elements to an array

One can also add new values to an existing array using the **insert(argument 1, argument 2)** function, where *argument 1* and *argument 2* must be the respective index (i.e. position in the array) of the new element and the value of the new element. This function is mainly used when one or more new values need to be added to an array and the position needs to be determined.

```
# inserting array using insert() function
a.insert(6, 60)
print ("Array after insertion : ", end =" ")
for i in (a):
    print (i, end =" ")
print()
```

You can also use the function **append(argument 1)** to add new values to an existing array. However, here you cannot specify the position, i.e. the index of the new value. The new element is simply appended to the end of the array.

```
# adding an element using append()
b.append(8.4)
print ("Array after insertion : ", end =" ")
for i in (b):
    print (i, end =" ")
print()
```

Overall example:

File Edit Format Run Options Window Help

```
# Adding Elements to a Array

# importing "array" module for array creations
import array as arr

# array with int type
a = arr.array('i', [10, 20, 30, 40, 50])
print ("Array before insertion : ", end =" ")
for i in range (0, 5):
    print (a[i], end =" ")
print()

# inserting array using insert() function
a.insert(6, 60)
print ("Array after insertion : ", end =" ")
for i in (a):
    print (i, end =" ")
print()

# array with float type
b = arr.array('d', [1.5, 2,4, 3.6, 4.6, 5.4])
print ("Array before insertion : ", end =" ")
for i in range (0, 5):
    print (b[i], end =" ")
print()

# adding an element using append()
b.append(8.4)
print ("Array after insertion : ", end =" ")
for i in (b):
    print (i, end =" ")
print()
```

Output:

```
Array before insertion :  10 20 30 40 50
Array after insertion :  10 20 30 40 50 60
Array before insertion :  1.5 2.0 4.0 3.6 4.6
Array after insertion :  1.5 2.0 4.0 3.6 4.6 5.4 8.4
>>> |
```

5.2.3 Access to elements of an array

As mentioned before, you can access a specific value of an array using the index. One uses the index number together with the index operator as in the following example:

Example:

File Edit Format Run Options Window Help

```
# [illegible]

import array as arr
a = arr.array('i', [10, 20, 30, 40, 50, 60])

# [illegible]
print("First Element: ", a[0])

# [illegible]
print("Third Element: ", a[2])
```

Output:

```
First Element:  10
Third Element:  30
>>> |
```

5.2.4 Removing elements from the array

A specific value of an array can be removed from an array with the **remove(argument 1)** function, where *argument 1* is the element to be removed. The position does not have to be specified here, since the element is characterized by the value. However, if the specified value is not present, an error is returned.

5.2.5 Division of an array

With the help of a slice operation (which is not a function in the actual sense in Python) you can define a certain range of an array, e.g. to display it. This works as follows with the help of a colon:

1) Use *array_name*[:*index_value*] to select elements from the beginning to a specified index value (*index_value*).

2) Using *array_name*[*index_value*:] to select elements only from a certain index value (*index_value*) to the end of the array.

3) Use *array_name*[*startindex* : *endindex*] to select elements within a defined index range.

Example:

File Edit Format Run Options Window Help

```
import array as arr

l = [10, 20, 30, 40, 50, 60, 70, 80, 90, 100]

a = arr.array('i', l)
print("Initial Array: ")
for i in (a):
    print(i, end =" ")

Sliced_array = a[4:9]
print("\nSlicing elements in a range 4-9: ")
print(Sliced_array)

Sliced_array = a[5:]
print("\nElements sliced from 5th "
      "element till the end: ")
print(Sliced_array)

Sliced_array = a[:]
print("\nPrinting all elements using slice operation: ")
print(Sliced_array)
```

Output:

```
Initial Array:
10 20 30 40 50 60 70 80 90 100
Slicing elements in a range 4-9:
array('i', [50, 60, 70, 80, 90])

Elements sliced from 5th element till the end:
array('i', [60, 70, 80, 90, 100])

Printing all elements using slice operation:
array('i', [10, 20, 30, 40, 50, 60, 70, 80, 90, 100])
>>>
```

5.2.6 Search element in an array

The **index(argument)** function is used to search for a specific element in an array. As output you get back the index of the first value which is identical to the entered "argument".

Example:

```
File  Edit  Format  Run  Options  Window  Help
# [illegible]

# [illegible]
import array

# [illegible]
arr = array.array('i', [10, 20, 30, 40, 50, 60])

# [illegible]
print ("The new created integer array is : ", end ="")
for i in range (0, 6):
    print (arr[i], end =" ")

print ("\r")

# [illegible]
print ("The index of 1st occurrence of 20 is : ", end ="")
print (arr.index(20))

# [illegible]
print ("The index of 1st occurrence of 60 is : ", end ="")
print (arr.index(60))
```

Output:

```
The new created integer array is : 10 20 30 40 50 60
The index of 1st occurrence of 20 is : 1
The index of 1st occurrence of 60 is : 5
>>> |
```

5.2.7 Updating elements in an array

Updating array elements can be done simply by reassigning a new value to the desired index value of the array.

So e.g. by *array_name*[1] = 30. That means the value with the index "1" (Attention: This is the second value, because it is counted from 0) gets the new value "30".

Example:

File Edit Format Run Options Window Help

```
# update an element in array

# Creating an Array
import array
arr = array.array('i', [10, 20, 30, 40, 50, 60])

# printing original array
print ("Array before updation : ", end ="")
for i in range (0, 6):
    print (arr[i], end =" ")

print ("\r")

# updating a element in a array
arr[2] = 100
print("Array after updation : ", end ="")
for i in range (0, 6):
    print (arr[i], end =" ")
print()
```

Output:

```
Array before updation : 10 20 30 40 50 60
Array after updation : 10 20 100 40 50 60
>>> |
```

So much for arrays and how to deal with them.

What have we learned in this chapter? To elaborate, it can be briefly summarized as follows: With the help of an array several values can be stored one after the other in one element. Similar to a variable, but in a larger number and in only one array element. By the respective index then a certain stored value can be addressed. You can edit arrays with different functions, e.g. add values, remove values or select parts of an array for an output.

In the next chapter, we'll briefly look at strings before moving on to more basics like tuples, functions, operators, and others.

5.3 Strings (character string or string of characters)

A string can be defined quite simply as a certain sequence of characters, whereby a character can ultimately also be called a symbol. The computer cannot really do anything with these characters per se. Why? Because the basic principle of a PC is the so-called binary system, which is based on the two numbers "0" and "1". Communication in digital systems takes place with the help of these numbers or with the help of various combinations of these two numbers.

A computer system stores a string (sequence of characters) precisely also in this form, i.e. as a combination of ones and zeros within the framework of the binary system. The conversion of characters into such binary numbers is called **encoding,** while the inversion is called **decoding.** The most common encoding schemes used in Python are **ASCII** and **Unicode**. An important point here is the immutability of Python strings. This simply means that strings (character sequences) cannot be changed once they have been created.

5.3.1 Creation of a string

In Python, a string can be created by assigning a specific string to a variable. The string is enclosed by either single, double, or even triple quotes.

This means, for example, string_01 = "Welcome".
(double quotation mark)

But it would be just as possible to use e.g. string_02 = 'Welcome'.
(single quotation mark)

Identical also e.g. string_02 = '''Welcome'''
(triple quotation mark)

Simple example a):

File Edit Format Run Options Window Help

```
# Creation of Python String

# Creating a String with single Quotes
String_01 = 'Welcome to the python World'
print("String with the use of Single Quotes: ")
print(String_01)
```

Output to a):

```
String with the use of Single Quotes:
Welcome to the python World
```

Extensive example b):

File Edit Format Run Options Window Help

```
# [illegible]

# [illegible]
String_01 = 'Welcome to the python World'
print("String with the use of Single Quotes: ")
print(String_01)

# [illegible]
String_01 = "Hello Python"
print("\nString with the use of Double Quotes: ")
print(String_01)

# [illegible]
String_01 = '''The top 1 popular programming language of 2021. '''
print("\nString with the use of Triple Quotes: ")
print(String_01)

# [illegible]
String_01 = '''Hello
            Python
            World'''
print("\nCreating a multiline String: ")
print(String_01)
```

Output to b):

```
String with the use of Single Quotes:
Welcome to the python World

String with the use of Double Quotes:
Hello Python

String with the use of Triple Quotes:
The top 1 popular programming language of 2021.

Creating a multiline String:
Hello
            Python
            World
>>>
```

5.3.2 Accessing characters in a string

Each character of a string can be accessed relatively similarly to the array also here by the method of indexing. The method of negative indexing is also very practical in this context, which can be quite useful when accessing individual characters, since one starts with the index quasi backwards, i.e. from behind.

How can you understand this?

An index of -1 refers to the last character of the string. In the positive indexing method, this would be equivalent to index 10.

H	E	L	L	O	P	Y	T	H	O	N
0	1	2	3	4	5	6	7	8	9	10
-11	-10	-9	-8	-7	-6	-5	-4	-3	-2	-1

If we try to access an index that does not exist (here e.g. -12) we will get the error message: "**Index Error**". Also, the index should be an integer, otherwise the message: "**Type error**" will be displayed.

Example:

File Edit Format Run Options Window Help

```
# Python Program to Access characters of String

String_01 = "HelloPython"
print("Initial String: ")
print(String_01)

# Printing First character
print("\nFirst character of String is: ")
print(String_01[0])

# Printing Last character
print("\nLast character of String is: ")
print(String_01[-1])
```

Output:

```
Initial String:
HelloPython

First character of String is:
H

Last character of String is:
n
>>> |
```

5.3.3 Slicing of strings (character strings)

Similar to the slicing operation used in arrays, you can use such an operation on strings to access a specific range of characters in a string (if you don't remember it exactly, take another look at the previous lessons) or see the example:

Example:

File Edit Format Run Options Window Help

```
# [illegible]

# [illegible]
String_01 = "PythonWorld"
print("Initial String: ")
print(String_01)

# [illegible]
print("\nSlicing characters from 6-11: ")
print(String_01[6:11])

# [illegible]
print("\nSlicing characters between " +
    "3rd and 2nd last character: ")
print(String_01[3:-2])
```

Output:

```
Initial String:
PythonWorld

Slicing characters from 6-11:
World

Slicing characters between 3rd and 2nd last character:
honWor
>>> |
```

5.3.4 Deleting / updating strings

As mentioned at the beginning, updating strings or deleting one or more specific characters of a string is not allowed because the individual characters of a string created in Python cannot be changed individually. In fact, only overwriting the entire string, or deleting the entire string and recreating it, can solve this problem. We perform the deletion operation using the term **del** (short for delete).

Example a): Try to update a string

```
File  Edit  Format  Run  Options  Window  Help
# Python Program to Update character of a String

String_01 = "HelloPython"
print("Initial String: ")
print(String_01)

# Updating a character of the String
String_01[2] = 'p'
print("\nUpdating character at 2nd Index: ")
print(String_01)
```

Output a): Error, because not possible

```
Initial String:
HelloPython
Traceback (most recent call last):
  File "C:/Users/official/Documents/Python/10.py", line 8, in <module>
    String_01[2] = 'p'
TypeError: 'str' object does not support item assignment
>>> |
```

Example b): Update the entire string

File Edit Format Run Options Window Help

```
# Python Program to Update entire String

String_01 = "WelcomeToPython"
print("Initial String: ")
print(String_01)

# Updating a String
String_01 = "HelloPython"
print("\nUpdated String: ")
print(String_01)
```

Output b): String was overwritten

```
Initial String:
WelcomeToPython

Updated String:
HelloPython
>>> |
```

Example c): Attempt to delete a single character of a string

File Edit Format Run Options Window Help

```
# Python Program to Delete characters from a String

String_01 = "HelloPython"
print("Initial String: ")
print(String_01)

# Deleting a character of the String
del String_01[2]
print("\nDeleting character at 2nd Index: ")
print(String_01)
```

Output c): Error, because not possible

```
Initial String:
HelloPython
Traceback (most recent call last):
  File "C:/Users/official/Documents/Python/10.py", line 8, in <module>
    del String_01[2]
TypeError: 'str' object doesn't support item deletion
>>> |
```

Example d): Deleting a complete string

```
File  Edit  Format  Run  Options  Window  Help
# Python Program to Delete entire String

String_01 = "HelloPython"
print("Initial String: ")
print(String_01)

# Deleting a String with the use of del
del String_01
print("\nDeleting entire String: ")
print(String_01)
```

Output d): String was successfully deleted and thus no longer found → Error message→ Re-creation of the string possible

```
Initial String:
HelloPython

Deleting entire String:
Traceback (most recent call last):
  File "C:/Users/official/Documents/Python/10.py", line 10, in <module>
    print(String_01)
NameError: name 'String_01' is not defined
>>> |
```

5.3.5 Escape characters in a string

In Python, non-printable characters are called escape characters. These can, for example, affect the sentence structure, i.e. represent a line break. Such characters are represented with the backslash notation, i.e. these characters are preceded by a backslash. The backslash and the character must be within quotation marks (double, i.e. "..." or single, i.e. '...').

In this expression, for example, **\n** precedes a line break before the text immediately following it:

```
print("\nDeleting character at 2nd Index: ")
```

Some of the most important Escape Characters are listed here:

Backslash notation	Description
\a	Bell or alarm
\b	Backspace key
\cx or \C-x	Control-x (CTRL-x)
\e	Escape key (ESC)
\f	Form feed
\n	Line break
\r	Keyboard feed
\s	Space
\t	Tab key
\x	Character x

5.3.6 Special string operators

Operators are keywords that can be used to perform operations, as in mathematics, for example. Suppose the string variables **'a'** and **'b'** contain the strings 'Hey' and 'You', respectively.

Operator	Description	Example
+	Operator for addition	**a + b**, results in *HeyYou*
*	Operator for multiplication	**a*2**, results in *HeyHey*
[]	Extracts the character from the specified index	**a[1]**, yields *e*

[:]	Extracts the characters from the specified range	**a[1:2]**, yields *ey*
in	Returns "true" or "1" if a character exists in the specified string	H **in** a, results in *1*
not in	Returns true or "1" if a character does not exist in the given string	M **not in** a, results in *1*

Note: Remember that the index starts at "0" when counting. So the first character of a string has index "0", the second has index "1", and so on.

5.3.7 Special operator for formatting strings

The special operator "**%**" gives Python a very cool and unique feature. This special operator is used in Python as a formatting operator for strings. The usage of the string formatting operator is as follows:

Example:

```
print("My name is %s and weight is %d kg!" % ('mark', 50))
```

Output:

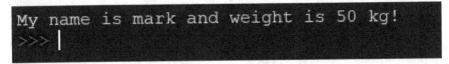

```
My name is mark and weight is 50 kg!
>>>
```

As we can see in the example, the **%** operator with a following letter or character - we will see which characters there are in a moment - is a kind of placeholder within a text or string, which also has a formatting function (depending on which letter we write after the **%**). With the following expression: **% ("mark", 50)** we then define which text or value we want.

Below is an overview of the characters that can be used together with the formatting operator.

Format icon	Conversion
%c	Characters
%s	Converting strings before formatting
%i or %d	decimal integer with sign
%u	Unsigned decimal integer
%o	octal integer
%x	hexadecimal integer
%X	hexadecimal integer
%e or %E	Exponential notation
%f	Floating point number

5.3.8 Arithmetic operators

Arithmetic operators are used in almost all programming languages. By the way, this name sounds more complicated than the thing is, because these are simply the symbols known from simple mathematics (i.e. "+" for the sum of two numbers, "*" for the multiplication of two numbers, etc.). In Python, there are the following arithmetic operators that can be used to perform mathematical operations:

1) For the addition +, e.g. x+y

2) For the subtraction -, e.g. x-y

3) For the multiplication *, e.g. x*y

4) For the division /, e.g. x/y

5) For the remainder of a division (modulo) %, e.g. x%y

6) For exponentiation **, e.g. x**y

7) For the smallest possible integer in the division (floor division) //, e.g. x//y

8) For a negative sign -, e.g. -y

9) For equality ==, so e.g. x == y (x and y will have the same values).

In this section we have learned what a string is and how we can handle it. In addition, we have dealt with escape characters and operators. In the next chapter we will first deal with the so-called "tuples" and then we will come to the functions.

5.4 Tuple

A tuple is simply a collection of values. The individual values are separated from each other by commas. In contrast to a variable, which stores one content, tuples can store many contents unchangeably. In other programming languages this would be called constants. You can store not only one content in tuples, but even several, which are then separated by commas. You can store unique and unchangeable values in them, such as the name and year of birth of a person.

Example a):

File Edit Format Run Options Window Help

```
tuple1 = ('mark', 'John', 2005, 2000);
tuple2 = (1, 2, 3, 4, 5 );
tuple3 = "a", "b", "c", "d";
```

Output a):

```
('mark', 'John', 2005, 2000)
(1, 2, 3, 4, 5)
('a', 'b', 'c', 'd')
>>>
```

You can also assign only one content to a tuple, in which case you must add a comma after the scalar value, such as in the following. If you forget the comma, Python would treat the value as a string.

Example b):

File Edit Format Run Options Window Help

```
tuple1 = (10,);
print(tuple1)
```

Output b):

```
(10,)
>>> |
```

Besides, it is also possible to create an empty tuple. This is possible by not specifying content between the brackets.

Example c):

File Edit Format Run Options Window Help

```
# An empty tuple
empty_tuple = ()
print (empty_tuple)
```

Output c):

```
()
>>> |
```

5.4.1 Concatenation of tuples

Two tuples can be concatenated or joined using the "+" operator as in the following example (analogous to mathematical addition).

Example:

File Edit Format Run Options Window Help

```
# Code for concatenating 2 tuples

tuple1 = (0, 1, 2, 3)
tuple2 = ('python', 'World')

# Concatenating above two
print(tuple1 + tuple2)
```

Output:

```
(0, 1, 2, 3, 'python', 'World')
>>> |
```

5.4.2 Nesting of tuples

Tuples can also be nested in Python as in the following example.

Example:

File Edit Format Run Options Window Help

```
# Code for creating nested tuples

tuple1 = (0, 1, 2, 3)
tuple2 = ('python', 'World')
tuple3 = (tuple1, tuple2)
print(tuple3)
```

Output:

```
((0, 1, 2, 3), ('python', 'World'))
>>> |
```

5.4.3 Repetitions in tuples

Tuples can be multiplied or repeated for a desired number of values using the "*" operator, as in the following example (analogous to mathematical multiplication).

Example:

File Edit Format Run Options Window Help

```
# Code to create a tuple with repetition

tuple3 = ('python',)*3
print(tuple3)
```

Output:

```
('python', 'python', 'python')
>>> |
```

5.4.4 Invariability of tuples

As defined at the beginning, tuples in Python are immutable (similar to strings). So if you try to assign individual elements to a tuple by using an index, the Python interpreter will give an error message.

Example: Try to update a tuple:

File Edit Format Run Options Window Help

```
#code to test that tuples are immutable

tuple1 = (0, 1, 2, 3)
tuple1[0] = 4
print(tuple1)
```

Output: Error message, because not possible:

```
Traceback (most recent call last):
  File "C:/Users/official/Documents/Python/11.py", line 4, in <module>
    tuple1[0] = 4
TypeError: 'tuple' object does not support item assignment
>>> |
```

5.4.5 Division of tuples

As with arrays, tuples can also be subjected to a slicing operation (splitting). Slicing is done in a similar way as with arrays, using ":" and specifying the index or range.

Example:

File Edit Format Run Options Window Help

```
# code to test slicing

tuple1 = (0 ,1, 2, 3, 4, 5)
print(tuple1[1:])
print(tuple1[::-1])
print(tuple1[2:4])
```

Output:

```
(1, 2, 3, 4, 5)
(5, 4, 3, 2, 1, 0)
(2, 3)
>>> |
```

5.4.6 Deleting elements in a tuple

Tuples, like strings, have the property of immutability, so individual elements of a given tuple cannot be deleted. Here, as with strings, the entire tuple must be deleted and, if necessary, recreated with the new or correct values.

A tuple can be deleted in an analogous way again with the **del** command.

Example:

File Edit Format Run Options Window Help

```
# Code for deleting a tuple

tuple1 = ('Mark', 'John', 2005, 2000)
print (tuple1)
del tuple1
print("After deleting tuple : ")
print(tuple1);
```

Output: Error message, because tuple is no longer defined:

```
('Mark', 'John', 2005, 2000)
After deleting tuple :
Traceback (most recent call last):
  File "C:/Users/official/Documents/Python/11.py", line 7, in <module>
    print(tuple1);
NameError: name 'tuple1' is not defined
>>> |
```

5.4.7 Predefined functions for tuples

In Python, you can use the following predefined functions to work with tuples. We'll take a closer look at what this means in a moment, using **len(tuple)** as an example.

Function	Description
cmp(tuple1, tuple2)	Compares the elements of two tuples
len(tuple)	Specifies the length of a tuple
max(tuple)	Returns the largest element (max. value) of the tuple
min(tuple)	Returns the smallest element (min. value) of the tuple
Tuple(seq)	Converts a list into a tuple

Let's take a detailed look at the procedure using the example of **len(tuple).** The command **len** (abbreviation for length) can be used to determine the length of a tuple, as can be seen in the table. The result is a number that indicates the number of values contained in a tuple, which is called length in the programming language.

Example:

File Edit Format Run Options Window Help

```
# Code for printing the length of a tuple

tuple1 = (0, 1, 2, 3, 4, 5)
print(len(tuple1))
```

Output:

```
6
>>>
```

6 Functions

In this section, let's talk about the functions that we can use in Python. A function can be defined in programming in general as a script or a collection of instructions that has the goal of executing a predefined procedure. As a developer, you can place a number of instructions in a function and call the respective function on demand by a defined command. This means that you do not always have to write the script of instructions from scratch, but this is stored in the function and can be called.

You can distinguish between 3 types of functions in Python:

1) Predefined functions, e.g. **print(...)**, **help(...)**

2) User-defined functions, i.e. functions you have created yourself.

3) Anonymous functions (also lambda function), i.e. function defined without a name.

In the following sections we will focus on **user-defined functions**, i.e. the procedure for creating your own functions.

6.1 Defining a Function

Depending on which instructions or which goal you want to execute with a function, you have to build the content of the respective function accordingly. Below are the basic steps and rules for defining a function. Later, of course, we will look at examples and how to work with functions.

1) To create a function you need the name **def** followed by the name of the function and two brackets followed by a colon, e.g. **def function_01 ()** :

2) You can write variables inside the brackets if you need them in the function. If you have more than one variable, you should separate them with commas, e.g. **def function_02 (name)** : or **def function_03(name, age)** : ("**name**" and "**age**" are already defined variables in our code).

3) The first statement of a function is called **docstring** and this describes what the function does. This is optional and we will come back to it in a moment.

4) The following actual code of the function, starts with a colon. There must also be an indentation between the line where the definition of the function begins (**def**).

5) At the end of the function the command **return** should be placed, the Python interpreter then leaves the function. Optionally, you can also have a value returned here. This desired value (e.g. a variable) must then be placed after **return.** But we will come back to this in a moment.

Example:

File Edit Format Run Options Window Help

```
# A simple Python function

def functionName():
  print("Welcome to Python")
```

Example:

File Edit Format Run Options Window Help

```
def function_name(parameters):
    """docstring"""
    statement(s)
    return expression
```

6.2 Docstring

The very first string (or text) after the function name is called a **docstring**, as has already been briefly mentioned. Docstrings can be seen simply as a kind of instruction for the user to represent the functionality of a certain function. This increases the readability of the code.

Example:

File Edit Format Run Options Window Help

```python
# A simple Python function to check whether x is even or odd

def evenOdd(x):
    """Function to check if the number is even or odd"""

    if (x % 2 == 0):
        print("even")
    else:
        print("odd")


# Driver code to call the function
print(evenOdd.__doc__)
```

Output:

```
Function to check if the number is even or odd
>>> |
```

6.3 The return statement

The **return** statement is used - as already briefly mentioned - to exit a function. In addition, the return statement can be used to return a specific value. Such values may be a result produced by the execution of statements within the function, or a value returned to ensure that a particular function has been successfully executed. The **return** statement can be either a variable, an expression, or a constant.

Example:

File Edit Format Run Options Window Help

```python
def square_value(value):
    """This function returns the square
    value of the entered number"""
    return value**2


print(square_value(2))
print(square_value(-4))
```

Output:

```
4
16
>>> |
```

6.4 Calling a function

Once a function has been defined, it can be called by using the function name followed by enclosed brackets, e.g. by **function_01()**

Example:

File Edit Format Run Options Window Help

```
# A simple Python function

def functionName():
  print("Welcome to Python")

# calling a function
functionName()
```

Output:

```
Welcome to Python
>>> |
```

6.5 Arguments of a Function

Function arguments are the "values" that are enclosed in the parentheses when a function is defined, for example, **def function_03 (name, age) :** "**name**" and "**age**". These arguments mainly fall into the following four categories:

1. Required arguments

If you want to call a previously defined function that contains arguments, you must make sure that the arguments are present in the correct order and number when the function is called, i.e. exactly as in the definition of the function.

The following example shows what happens if you do not specify the argument (**str**) when calling the **printme()** function:

Example a), argument forgotten when calling:

File Edit Format Run Options Window Help

```
# Function definition is here

def printme( str ):
   "This prints a passed string into this function"
   print(str)
   return;

# Now you can call printme function
printme()
```

Output a), error message because argument is missing:

```
Traceback (most recent call last):
  File "C:/Users/official/Documents/Python/11.py", line 8, in <module>
    printme()
TypeError: printme() missing 1 required positional argument: 'str'
>>> |
```

2. Keyword arguments

Keyword arguments are used in Python to place arguments out of order when calling a function. The Python interpreter has the option to use the keyword specified in the function call and match the respective argument with the corresponding parameter in the function definition.

Example b):

File Edit Format Run Options Window Help

```python
# Function definition is here

def printme( str ):
    "This prints a passed string into this function"
    print(str)
    return;

# Now you can call printme function
printme( str = "My string")
```

Output b):

```
My string
>>>
```

Example c):

File Edit Format Run Options Window Help

```python
# Function definition is here

def printinfo( name, age ):
    "This prints a passed info into this function"
    print("Name: ", name)
    print("Age ", age)
    return;

# Now you can call printinfo function
printinfo( age=30, name="John" )
```

Output c):

```
Name:  John
Age  30
>>>
```

3. Standard arguments

Default arguments are used in Python functions when a default value must be assigned to an argument. So you can use them to make an argument equal to a predefined default value.

Example d):

File Edit Format Run Options Window Help

```
# Function definition is here

def printinfo( name, age = 50 ):
    "This prints a passed info into this function"
    print("Name: ", name)
    print("Age ", age)
    return;

# Now you can call printinfo function
printinfo( age=60, name="mark" )
printinfo( name="john" )
```

Output d):

```
Name:  mark
Age  60
Name:  john
Age  50
>>> |
```

4. Arguments of variable length

One uses the following procedure when one needs to execute a function for more than the number of arguments defined in the function definition. Such additional arguments are called variable length arguments and need not have been defined in the function definition. An asterisk "*" is placed in front of the variable name containing the values of the variable length arguments for this purpose. This variable length argument remains empty if no additional arguments were named during the function call.

Example e):

File Edit Format Run Options Window Help

```
# Function definition is here

def printinfo( arg1, *vartuple ):
   "This prints a variable passed arguments"
   print("Output is: ")
   print(arg1)
   for var in vartuple:
      print(var)
   return;

# Now you can call printinfo function
printinfo( 1 )
printinfo( 5, 6, 7 )
```

Output (e):

```
Output is:
1
Output is:
5
6
7
>>> |
```

6.6 Pass by reference

It is important to emphasize that in Python almost all variable names automatically become references ("pass by reference"). This means that whenever a variable is passed to a function, a new reference to the object is created. This process is very similar to passing by reference in Java programming.

Example a):

File Edit Format Run Options Window Help

```
def myFunction(x):
    x[0] = 20


lst = [1, 2, 3, 4, 5, 6]
myFunction(lst)
print(lst)
```

Output a):

```
[20, 2, 3, 4, 5, 6]
>>>
```

In addition, it is important to know that if a variable is passed to a specific function and the entire reference is changed to another, the connection between the reference and the passed variable is broken.

Example b):

File Edit Format Run Options Window Help

```
def myFunction(x):

    # After below line link of x with previous
    # object gets broken. A new object is assigned
    # to x.
    x = [20, 30, 40]


# Driver Code (Note that lst is not modified
# after function call.
lst = [1, 2, 3, 4, 5, 6]
myFunction(lst)
print(lst)
```

Output b):

```
[1, 2, 3, 4, 5, 6]
>>>
```

7 Loops and Conditions

In the previous examples, we have already used or accepted loops and conditions, such as the expressions **for** (loop) or **if** (condition), several times without knowing exactly what is actually happening here. Since loops and conditions are very basic operations of any programming language and code, we will look at them in detail below.

7.1 Loops

7.1.1 While loop

In all programming languages, a while loop can be used to execute a series of statements repeatedly, i.e. over and over again, until a certain condition is no longer met. Once the certain condition is no longer met (**False**), the execution of the loop is stopped and then the statements of the next lines of code are executed. For example, we can add a "1" to the variable "i" (initial value = 0) until the value of "i" would become greater than 3. So, the loop or the addition of this loop should be stopped when "i" reaches the value "3". This would then look like this:

Example:

```
i=0

while i<4:
    print("Iteratino Number: %d"%i)
    i=i+1

print("\nThe while loop ended")
```

Output:

```
Iteration Number: 0
Iteration Number: 1
Iteration Number: 2
Iteration Number: 3

The while loop ended
```

Be sure to also note the colon and indentations!

7.1.2 For loop

Just like a while loop, a for loop can be used to execute statements repeatedly. The difference to a while loop is that a for loop runs until a defined range is over and the for loop does not check whether a condition is still **true** or **false**. Simply put, you can use a for loop to repeat a series of statements over a range of values, so for example :

Example:

```
for i in range(0,5):
    print("Iteration Number: %d"%i)

print("\nThe for loop ended")

```

Output:

```
Iteration Number: 0
Iteration Number: 1
Iteration Number: 2
Iteration Number: 3
Iteration Number: 4

The for loop ended
```

As you can see in the example, the execution of the for loop stops as soon as the iteration would leave the specified value range (0 - 5). Then, as with the while loop, the command of the next line of code is executed.

7.2 Conditions

In almost all programming languages - and of course in life in general - decision making plays an important role. Decisions can be made in programming generally by given conditions logically and automatically by the program. Conditional statements check whether certain predefined conditions are met or not. There are several types of conditional statements in Python:

7.2.1 If statement

The **if** statement is the most basic conditional statement in Python. An if statement simply checks whether a given condition is **true** or **false**, and executes certain commands if the condition is **true**, depending on the condition. For example, one could define that a ripe apple must be red. An if statement could then be used to check whether this condition is true for a particular apple on a tree. If the condition is true, one must then determine what should happen (e.g. include the command that the picking process should be started).

The following example illustrates the functionality of the if statement once again in program code.

Example:

```
i=2

if i==2:
    print("condition met")
```

Output:

```
condition met
>>>
```

As you can see, the value of "**i**" is equal to "2" and therefore the conditional statement becomes true and the script executes the given statement corresponding to the condition.

7.2.2 else statement

The **else statement** is used in all cases where both the true and false results of checking a condition are to be taken into account. That is, in this case it is possible to determine which statements should be executed both in the true case (condition = **true**) and in the false case (condition = **false**).

Example:

```
i=2

if i==1:
    print("condition is true")
else:
    print("condition is false")
```

Output:

```
condition is false
>>>
```

7.2.3 elif statement

The elif **statement** is also known as elseif statement in other programming languages. The elif statement follows after an if statement and before an else statement, i.e. right in between. In this case, the normal (first) if condition is checked first to see if it is true or false. If it is true, the statement referring to the if-condition is executed and the check of the remaining elif- and else-conditions is not performed anymore. However, if the first if condition is **false,** the elif condition is checked. If this condition is also not true (**false**), the statement for the else condition is executed, otherwise (if the condition is true) the statement for elif is executed. So, in a way, the elif statement is a second if check after the first if check (but is only checked if the first if check was not true, i.e. false).

Example:

```
i=2

if i==1:
    print("condition is true")
elif i==2:
    print("the elif condition became true")
else:
    print("condition is false")
```

Output:

```
the elif condition became true
>>>
```

7.2.4 Nested if statement

To make it a bit more complex, you can now nest if statements inside each other in programming. However, a nested if statement is simply an if statement that is inside another if statement. Nested if statements are used in all cases where one or more additional conditions must be tested within the main condition. That is, both conditions (1st condition and 2nd condition) must be true for the complete condition to be true.

Example a):

```
i=2
j=1

if i==2:
    print("main condition met")
    if j==1:
        print("nested condition met")

else:
    print("main condition not met")
```

Output a):

```
main condition met
nested condition met
>>> |
```

In this example, we see that the main condition is true. Therefore, in the second step, the nested if condition was also checked and found to be true as well. That is, both conditions are satisfied and the statement specified in them is therefore executed.

In contrast, in the following example, the main condition is not met, so the second condition, which is a nested condition and actually true, is not even checked.

Example b):

```
i=1
j=1

if i==2:
    print("main condition met")
    if j==1:
        print("nested condition met")

else:
    print("main condition not met")
```

Output b):

```
main condition not met
>>>
```

7.2.5 The short-hand statements for if and else

The so-called shorthand if statement is used as a kind of abbreviated if statement. It can be used to quickly specify a single statement to be executed if the condition is **true.**

Example a):

```
i=1

if i==1: print ("condition met")
```

Output a):

```
condition met
>>> 
```

Analogously, this also works for the shorthand else statement:

Example b):

```
i=1

if i==1: print ("condition met")
else: print("condition not met")
```

Output b):

```
condition met
>>>
```

7.2.6 Logical operators

Logical operators are used to perform operations between operations. In Python, logical operators are mainly used with conditional statements that need to determine whether a particular condition is true or false based on two or more variable values. This provides an alternative to the nested if statements from one of the previous sections, for example.

There are three logical operators in Python:

Operator	Description	Syntax
and	True if both operands are true	x **and** y
or	True if one of the two operands is true	x **or** y
not	True if the operand is false	**not** x

Example:

```
i=1
j=2

if i==1 and j==2:
    print("the condition is true")

if i==1 or j==5:
    print("either one condition is true or both conditions are true")

if not j==1:
    print("j is not equal to 1")
```

Output:

```
the condition is true
either one condition is true or both conditions are true
j is not equal to 1
>>>
```

8 Other important basics in Python

8.1 Possibility to enter a text by a user

The Python environment also makes it possible to require user input. That is, the user can be given the ability to perform input in the form of letters and numbers. A program can be developed in such a way that it makes a decision based on user input or behaves in a certain way based on input. You can either prompt for input directly in Python, which will be the case if you are the user, or you can create a graphical interface for input, which is a bit more difficult and which we will get to later. The input prompt is implemented with the **input()** function.

Example:

```
username = input("Enter Your Name! ")
print("Hello "+username)
```

Output:

```
Enter Your Name! Andersen
Hello Andersen
>>>
```

8.2 Insert current date & time in Python

Python also has a pre-installed library called **datetime**. This library allows you to implement a system timestamp or a date stamp.

Example:

```
import datetime

current_date_time=datetime.datetime.now()
print(current_date_time)
```

Output:

```
2021-12-20 22:04:15.792415
>>>
```

8.3 The try-except statement and its use

The **try-except statement** is, in very simple terms, a built-in mechanism for handling errors or exceptions. The **try statement** internally checks the code that follows it for errors. When an error occurs, the code predefined in the **except statement is** executed to handle or fix the error instead of printing a nasty error message. The try-except statement should therefore be implemented for programs that need to execute continuously without interruption or error messages when an error occurs.

However, let's take a look at this as well, using an example that is perhaps a little easier to understand. In the following example, the exception (except) of the try-except statement occurred because the value of x was not assigned at the beginning. Normally, an error message would appear. In this case, however, the code defined in the exception clause (except) is executed.

Example:

```
try:
    print(x)
except:
    print("An exception occured in printing the value of x")
```

Output:

```
An exception occured in printing the value of x
```

9 Basics of object-oriented programming (OOP)

Before we get to know the practical workings of OOP in the next chapters, we will first briefly familiarize ourselves with the theoretical background of object-oriented programming (OOP) in this section, in order to then better understand the concrete workings.

The central element in object-oriented programming is the class. In addition to the class, there are also objects, attributes (properties) and functions (methods). Each class has both attributes and functions. In the following, let's look at a human being or a person, for example, for better understanding. The definition human or person represents our class. A concrete person would then be our object (e.g. the person: Jim). Each person has attributes or properties, these are e.g. age, gender, name or other. The properties themselves (age, sex, name) are the attributes of a class (in our case the class: human). Every human being has these attributes, but the concrete expression is different for different people. Jim, for example, is 30 years old (attribute: age) and male (attribute: gender) and is called Jim (attribute: name). However, Jim does not only have attributes, but he can also do something. Jim can, for example, "eat", but he can also "walk" or, for example, something more complex like: "play tennis". These abilities would be called methods in OOP.

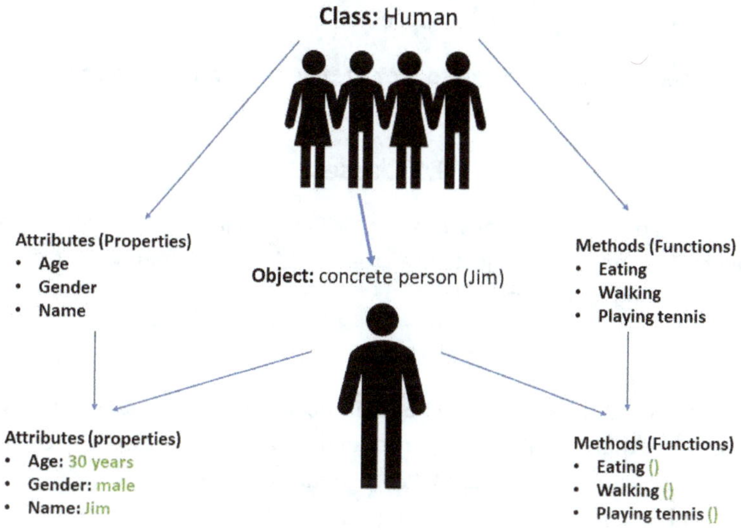

In object-oriented programming, such classes (e.g., our Jim) are used to develop larger and more complex software programs, because classes are reusable in OOP.

For the sake of clarity, what we discussed in the previous paragraph can be summarized again as follows:

Class

So to speak, the generic term for our objects. For example, a car would be called a class. The concrete car model with its own chassis number and associated specific individual equipment of a brand, on the other hand, would be an object.

Object

Instances of classes created with specially defined data. For example, a concrete car model of a brand with specific chassis number (or individual equipment).

Method (= function)

Functions defined within classes (car) that describe the behavior or functionality of an object (specific car model). So e.g. "driving", "flashing", "honking".

Attribute (= property)

Attributes reflect the state or properties of an object. The totality of attributes (the color of a car, or the number of doors) make an object (specific car model), which is subject to a common class (automobile), unique.

In the next section we would like to look at object-oriented programming in the practical way of working.

9.1 Classes

As we discussed in the previous chapter, a Python class can be defined as an umbrella term from which objects are created. Most importantly, a class allows you to bundle data and functionality.

Defining a class creates a new object of a particular class type that can be used to create instances that inherit the properties of the same class. A class creates a user-defined data structure that contains its own data elements and member functions. This data and functions can be accessed by creating an instance of this class.

Important rules related to classes in Phyton are:

1) Classes are created with the **class** keyword.

2) Variables that belong to classes are called **attributes.**

3) Attributes are global, i.e. they can be accessed with the dot operator "**.**" operator.

For example, for *Myclass.Myattribute*, "*Myclass*" would be the name of the class and "*Myattribute*" would be the name of the attribute.

9.2 The definition of a class

The definition of a class is very simple and runs in a similar - but different - way to functions. You don't use **def** here, but **class,** followed by the class name and a colon. Here, for example, the class object "*cars*" is defined:

File Edit Format Run Options Window Help

```
# demonstrate defining a class

class cars:
    pass
```

9.3 Objects of a class

As we already know, an object can be defined as a child instance of a particular class. This means that an object is an entity with a unique set of attributes (properties) of that class.

The **state** of an object is represented by its attributes (object properties: "red", "large").

The **behavior** of an object is represented by its methods (functions like "blink", "honk"). It also reflects the reaction of an object to other objects.

The **identity** of an object is determined by a unique name (e.g. "Jim") and allows an object to interact with other objects.

9.4 Declaring / Instantiating objects

When a particular object (e.g. "Jim") of a class (e.g. "Human") is created, it is called instantiation. All instances of a certain class have the same attributes ("**color**:", "**size**:") and the behavior of the class. However, the respective individual values of the attributes ("Color: **red**", "Size: **large**") make each object unique.

A single class can have any number of instances (individual objects).

In Python, an object can be defined, or rather instantiated, simply as follows.

Example:

```
class cars:
    print("An object has been created from class called 'cars'")

object1=cars()
```

Output:

```
An object has been created from class called 'cars'
>>>
```

The keyword "self"

Class methods have an additional first parameter called "**self**" in the method definition. When calling the method, it is not necessary to specify an argument or a value. To understand this better, let's look at the following scenario:

Suppose a class **myclass** has an object called **myobject** and a method called **mymethod** with two arguments **arg1** and **arg2** at the method definition. If we call the mymethod method of a particular object as follows,

myobject.mymethod (arg1, arg2)

the Python interpreter automatically converts the method call of a given object into the following form:

myclass.mymethod(myobject, arg1, arg2)

9.5 The "__init__" method

If you have ever worked with or have basic knowledge of C++ or Java, you may see the **__init__** method as similar to constructors in C++ or Java. But don't worry, if you don't have any previous knowledge in other programming languages, we will also develop a clear idea of the **__init__** method through the following explanation.

This method or constructor (**__init__**) is simply used to initialize the state of an object. This means that the main purpose of the **__init__** method is to create the initial state for objects (initialization). Similar to other methods, a constructor consists of a collection of statements that are executed when an object is created. That is, the **__init__** method is executed as soon as the object is declared by the class.

Example:

File Edit Format Run Options Window Help

```
# A Sample class with init method
class Person:

    # init method or constructor
    def __init__(self, name):
        self.name = name

    # Sample Method
    def say_hi(self):
        print('Hello, my name is', self.name)

p = Person('Mark')
p.say_hi()
```

Output:

```
Hello, my name is Mark
>>> |
```

10 GUI Development with Python

The abbreviation **GUI** stands for "Graphical User Interface". In Python, we have the possibility to develop a professional-looking command prompt (GUI) for our programs. This can be, for example, a window for selecting certain options:

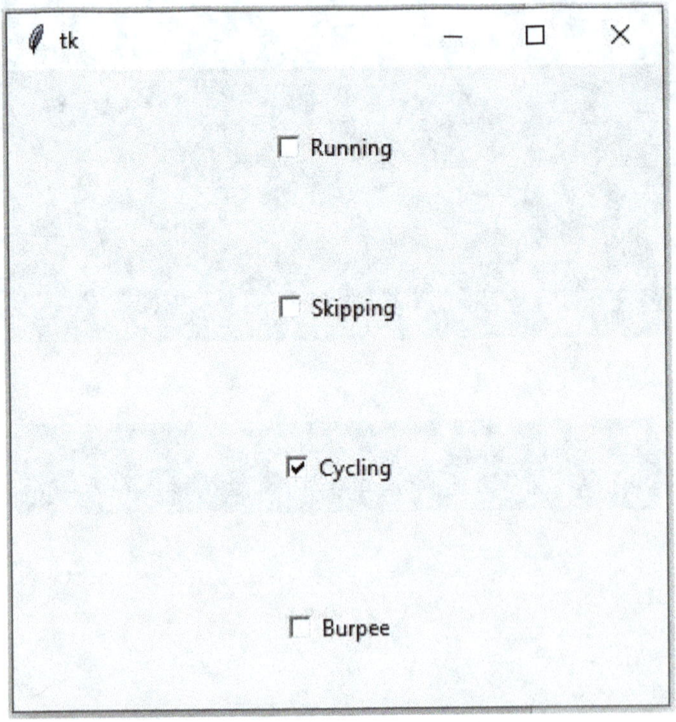

or even a clickable button:

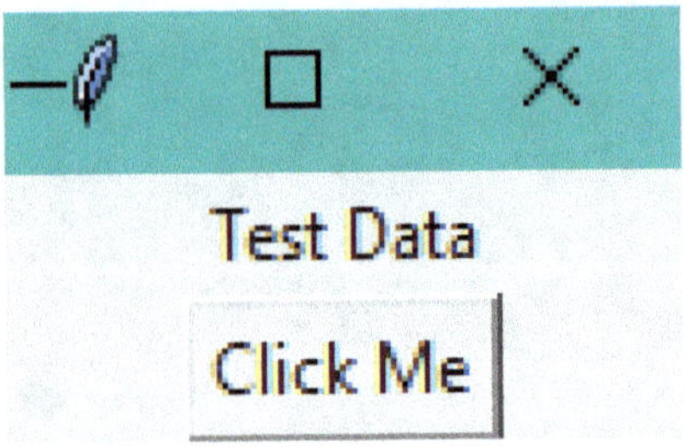

We will look at how to create such a GUI in this chapter. There are several options or modules / packages available in the Python environment for creating GUIs:

1) Tkinter

2) wxPython

3) JPython

However, we will deal exclusively with Python's Tkinter library module for GUI development in this chapter.

10.1 The Tkinter GUI development package/library

Tkinter is the default built-in GUI library package for the Python environment. With this module it is quite easy to create user-friendly GUIs with a great look and feel, as the combination of Python and Tkinter makes it very easy for us, as we will see in a moment. At the same time, it is very interesting to know that a GUI developed with Tkinter can run on the Windows operating system, as well as on macOS, Linux, etc. The Tkinter GUI applications look like they belong to the operating system platform itself, since they are rendered natively.

Creating a GUI application

To be able to create a GUI application with Tkinter, you have to go through several (relatively simple) steps, which are listed below:

1) Import Tkinter module (with **import ... as**).

2) Create a main window for the GUI application.

3) Add widgets (buttons, selection fields, ...) to the GUI application - depending on possible user input.

4) Create an event loop to perform actions for each event triggered by the user.

The first two steps are implemented as follows:

```
import tkinter as tk # Importing the Tkinter module
window = tk.Tk() # Creating the main window
```

You will then get the following (still empty) main window as output:

10.2 Tkinter widgets

In order to fill the still empty main window with meaningful elements and to create a nice GUI in this way, Tkinter offers a variety of widgets. These can be divided into control elements and information elements. Tkinter offers various control elements such as buttons, text fields, radio buttons, dropdown menus, etc. Also some information elements like labels, color indicators and so on. We will take a look at the most important widgets below.

10.2.1 Button

A button widget is used to insert a clickable button into the GUI application window. One can also display a text on the button so that the purpose of the button can be clearly conveyed. The function to be executed or called when this button is pressed can be assigned both when the button is declared and at a later time.

You can create such a button using the following statement and syntax:

```
w = Button ( master, option=value, ... )
```

The parameters are to be understood as follows:

Master is needed for the reference to the GUI main window (in our case the still empty GUI window). Here the name that was used in the definition is entered (in the previous one e.g. window was used). This way Python knows in which GUI window the button should be placed.

With *Option* you determine the properties of the button, e.g. the background color or the height of the buttons. If there are several properties, each property and its desired value are separated from each other by commas - starting from the second digit after the *master*.

Probably the most commonly used options / properties of buttons are:

Option	**Description**
command	Function that is called when the button is clicked on
font	Button font
bg	Background color
height	Height of the button in text lines or pixels
bd	Width of the button border in pixels (2 by default).
activebackground	Background color when the mouse cursor is on the button
activeforeground	Foreground color when the mouse cursor is on the button

Methods or functions for Buttons:

To make sure that something happens when the user clicks on the button, you need methods. For the button element there are two methods that are often used:

1) flash()

In this method the button flashes back and forth between the active and normal state colors several times, so that the button attracts the user's attention.

2) invoke()

This method calls the callback function of the button and returns what the function should perform. If there is no callback for the button, no action is performed. But let's take a look at this right now with an example.

Before that, we need to know what the **pack()** method does. With this method, simply put, you can organize widgets into blocks.

Example:

```
from tkinter import* #Importing all packages from Tkinter
import tkinter as tk

def show_text():
    messagel.config(text='Test Data') #Changing the text label


root = tk.Tk() # Creating the main window

#Declaring the label
messagel=Label(root, text = 'Display Data')
messagel.pack()

#Declaring the button
buttonl=Button(root, text = 'Click Me', command = show_text)
buttonl.pack()

mainloop()
```

Output: before clicking the button

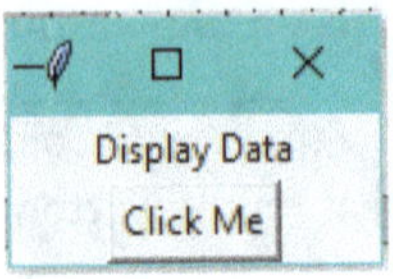

Output: after clicking the button

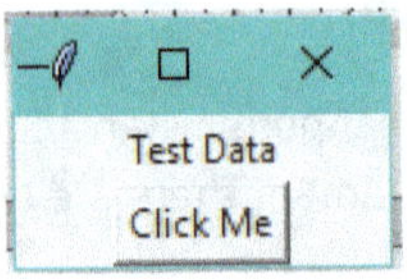

10.2.2 Canvas (graphic area)

A canvas is simply a rectangular graphical area that can be placed in a GUI window to display layouts, images, graphics, text, or anything else.

The parameters are similar to the buttons as follows:

Master is again needed for the reference to the GUI main window (see Buttons).

With *Option* you again determine the properties of the graphic area, e.g. the dimensions or the background color. If there are several properties, each property and its desired value (=value) is also inserted here, separated by commas - starting from the second digit after the *master.*

Probably the most commonly used options / properties of buttons are:

Option	**Description**
heigth	Height of the graphic area (y-direction)
width	Width of the graphical area (x-direction)
bd	Width of the border in pixels (2 by default)
bg	Background color
cursor	Used cursor within the area (e.g. arrow, circle, ...)
confine	With *true it is* not possible to scroll outside the scrolling area

By default, the Canvas widget supports the following elements for graphing or drawing:

arc:

Creates an arc-shaped representation.

```
coord = 10, 50, 240, 210
arc = canvas.create_arc(coord, start=0, extent=150, fill="blue")
```

image:

Creates an image element (instance of the BitmapImage or PhotoImage classes).

```
filename = PhotoImage(file = "test.gif")
image = canvas.create_image(50, 50, anchor=NE, image=filename)
```

line:

Creates a line-shaped element.

```
line = canvas.create_line(x0, y0, x1, y1, ..., xn, yn, options)
```

oval:

Creates a circle or an ellipse at the specified coordinates. Two pairs of coordinates, namely the upper left and the lower right corner, are required for the definition.

```
oval = canvas.create_oval(x0, y0, x1, y1, options)
```

polygon:

Creates a polygon defined by three vertices.

```
polygon= canvas.create_polygon(x0,y0,x1,y1,...xN, yN, options)
```

Let's look at this with an example.

Example:

File Edit Format Run Options Window Help

```
import tkinter

top = tkinter.Tk()

C = tkinter.Canvas(top, bg="blue", height=300, width=250)

coord = 10, 50, 240, 210
arc = C.create_arc(coord, start=0, extent=230, fill="yellow")

C.pack()
top.mainloop()
```

Output:

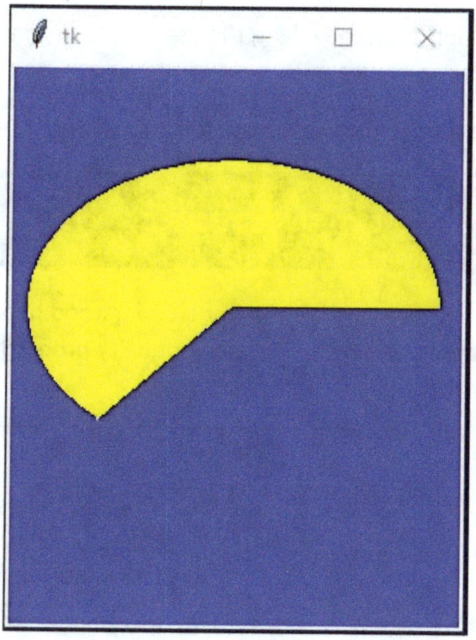

10.2.3 Check button widget (selection button)

With the help of a check button widget, the user of the program can select one or more options from given choices.

You can create such a selection button using the following statement and syntax:

```
w = Checkbutton ( master, option, ... )
```

The parameters *master* and *option* are to be understood here as in the previous sections. Probably the most commonly used options / properties of buttons in this case are:

Option	Description
command	Function call when the user selects or deselects a checkbutton
bd	Width of the border in pixels (2 by default)
bg	Background color
activebackground	Background color when the mouse cursor is on the button

Methods or functions for selection buttons:

When dealing with selection button elements, there are the following commonly used methods:

1) select()
This method can be used to check if the button is selected or checked.

2) deselect()
This method causes the button to be deselected if it was selected.

3) flash()
In this method, the button flashes back and forth between the active and normal state colors several times, so that the button attracts the user's attention.

4) invoke()

This method calls the callback function of the button and returns what the function should perform. If there is no callback for the button, no action is performed.

5) toggle()

This method can be used to toggle the status of the Select button. (e.g. : Delete if selected or Select if not selected).

Let's take a look at this, too, with the help of an example:

Example:

File Edit Format Run Options Window Help

```
from tkinter import *
import tkinter.messagebox
import tkinter

top = tkinter.Tk()
CheckVar1 = IntVar()
CheckVar2 = IntVar()
CheckVar3 = IntVar()
CheckVar4 = IntVar()

C1 = Checkbutton(top, text = "Running", variable = CheckVar1, \
                 onvalue = 1, offvalue = 0, height=5, \
                 width = 20)

C2 = Checkbutton(top, text = "Skipping", variable = CheckVar2, \
                 onvalue = 1, offvalue = 0, height=5, \
                 width = 20)

C3 = Checkbutton(top, text = "Cycling", variable = CheckVar3, \
                 onvalue = 1, offvalue = 0, height=5, \
                 width = 20)

C4 = Checkbutton(top, text = "Burpee", variable = CheckVar4, \
                 onvalue = 1, offvalue = 0, height=5, \
                 width = 20)

C1.pack()
C2.pack()
C3.pack()
C4.pack()
top.mainloop()
```

Output:

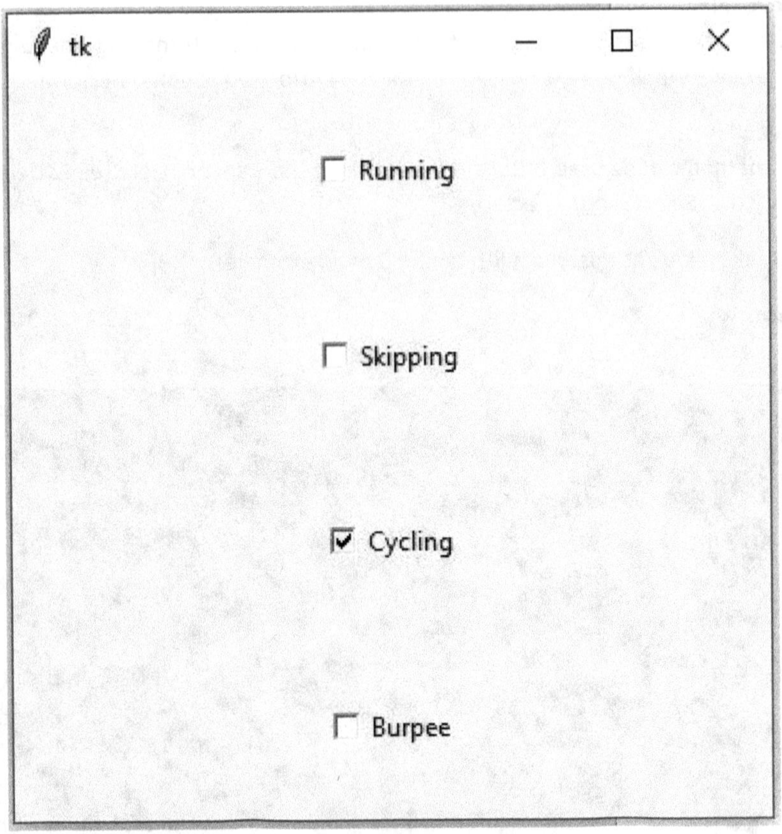

10.2.4 Entry widget (entry-widget)

The Input widget can be used to request or accept a single-line text (string) from a user. However, if you want to display multiple lines of text, it is better to use the Text widget.

Such an input field is created with the following statement and syntax:

```
w = Entry( master, option, ... )
```

The parameters *master* and *option* are again to be understood as in the previous sections. Probably the most frequently used options / properties of buttons in this case are:

Option	Description

bd	Width of the border in pixels (2 by default)
bg	Background color
font	Text font

Methods or functions for input buttons:

When dealing with input button element there are following two frequently used methods:

1) get()
This method returns the current content of the entry.

2) delete (first, last=none)
This method allows to delete characters from the widget, starting with the index number at the first (*first*) to the last (*last*) character. If the second argument is not specified, only a single character at the first index will be deleted.

Let's look at this again with an example:

Example:

File Edit Format Run Options Window Help

```
from tkinter import *

top = Tk()
L1 = Label(top, text="UserName")
L1.pack( side = LEFT)
E1 = Entry(top, bd =5)
E1.pack(side = RIGHT)

top.mainloop()
```

Output:

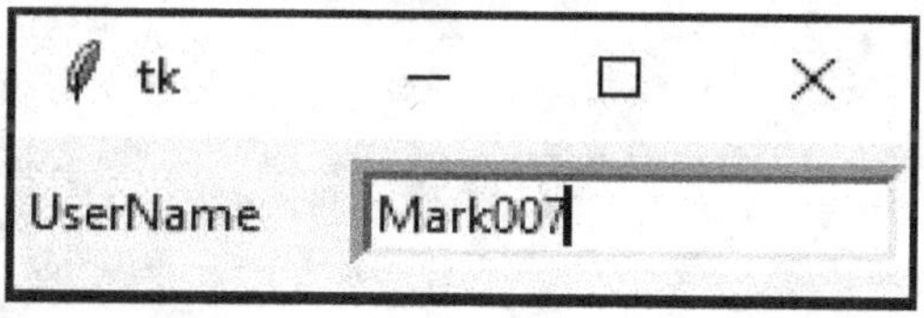

10.2.5 Frame widget (Frame widget)

The frame widget is important for grouping and organizing other widgets in a meaningful way. The frame widget simply acts as a kind of container that takes other widgets and places them all within a desired position in the main GUI window.

You can create such a frame with the following statement and syntax:

```
w = Frame ( master, option, ... )
```

The parameters *master* and *option* are again to be understood as in the previous sections. Probably the most frequently used options / properties of buttons in this case are:

Option	Description
bd	Width of the border in pixels (2 by default)
bg	Normal background color

Example:

File Edit Format Run Options Window Help

```
from tkinter import *

root = Tk()
frame = Frame(root)
frame.pack()

bottomframe = Frame(root)
bottomframe.pack( side = BOTTOM )

redbutton = Button(frame, text="Red", fg="red")
redbutton.pack( side = LEFT)

greenbutton = Button(frame, text="Brown", fg="brown")
greenbutton.pack( side = LEFT )

bluebutton = Button(frame, text="Blue", fg="blue")
bluebutton.pack( side = LEFT )

blackbutton = Button(bottomframe, text="Black", fg="black")
blackbutton.pack( side = BOTTOM)

root.mainloop()
```

Output:

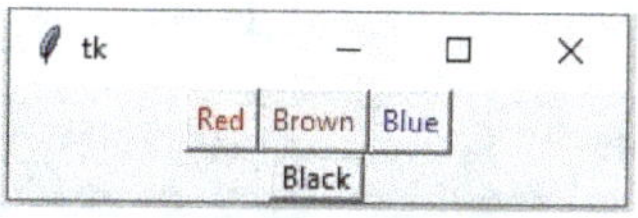

10.2.6 Label widget

This widget renders a display field where you can insert an image or text. The image or text can be updated at any time. This widget allows additional operations for the text it contains, such as underlining, bold, etc.

You can create such a label with the following statement and syntax:

```
w = Label ( master, option, ... )
```

As you can already imagine, *master* and *option* are again to be understood as in the previous sections. Probably the most commonly used options / properties of buttons in this case are:

Option	Description
anchor	To control the label position within the widget (if additional space is available).
text	To display one or more lines of text
bg	Background color

Example:

File Edit Format Run Options Window Help

```
from tkinter import *

root = Tk()
var = StringVar()
label = Label( root, textvariable=var, relief=RAISED )

var.set("Hey!? How are you doing?")
label.pack()
root.mainloop()
```

Output:

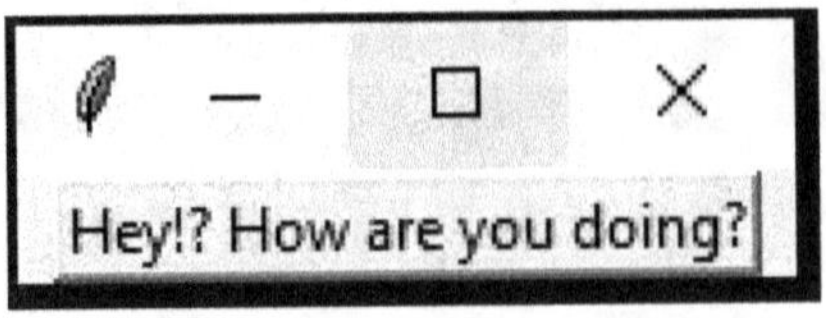
Hey!? How are you doing?

11 DIY projects

Now let's move on to the DIY projects to apply what we have learned and to deepen the theory.

11.1 Project 1: A simple calculator with user input

In this project we will write together and step by step a Python script for a simple calculator with basic arithmetic operations like addition, subtraction, division and multiplication.

Step 1: Open and save new empty Python script

First, we need to open a new Python script file and save it with a name. In the Python IDLE, you can click on the **File** menu and select **New File.** Now you have a new Python script file open, you can save it with a name of your choice by clicking on the **File** menu and then on the **Save** option.

File Edit Format Run Options Window Help

Step 2: Receiving user input

As discussed in the previous chapters, the user can be given an option to enter so that the user can enter two numbers and the operator (i.e., + or -, for example) to calculate the result.

```
value1=int(input("Enter the 1st value: "))
value2=int(input("Enter the 2nd value: "))
operator=input("Enter the arithmetic operator: ")
```

The two values entered by the user and the arithmetic operator are then stored in the variables named *value1*, *value2* and *operator.* In addition, the addition ***int*** converts the numbers entered into integers (this is necessary because the input is in the form of strings via the input prompt in Python).

Step 3: Implement conditional statements

To define the four desired arithmetic operations, we can then use conditional statements as follows:

```
if operator == "+":
    final_val = value1+value2

elif operator == "-":
    final_val = vlaue1-value2

elif operator == "/":
    final_val = value1/value2

elif operator =="*":
    final_val = value1*value2
```

Step 4: Continuous execution of the program

A mechanism should be implemented to run the program continuously, otherwise the program would run only once and then stop. We implement this with a simple while statement at the end of the code so that the program runs continuously.

```
while(1):
    calculator()
```

Below we see once again the complete Python script for the described project. In the script, the **calculator** function has been defined and all instructions have been placed inside the function so that the function in question can be executed continuously by calling it inside an infinite while loop that runs continuously.

```
def calculator():
    value1=int(input("Enter the 1st value: "))
    value2=int(input("Enter the 2nd value: "))
    operator=input("Enter the arithmetic operator: ")

    if operator == "+":
        final_val = value1+value2

    elif operator == "-":
        final_val = vlaue1-value2

    elif operator == "/":
        final_val = value1/value2

    elif operator =="*":
        final_val = value1*value2

    print(final_val)

while(1):
    calculator()
```

Here is the complete written code for a simple copy into the Python IDLE:

```
def calculator():

  value1=int(input("Enter the 1st value: "))

  value2=int(input("Enter the 2nd value: "))

  operator=input("Enter the arithmetic operator: ")


  if operator == "+":

    final_val = value1+value2


  elif operator == "-":

    final_val = value1-value2


  elif operator == "/":
```

```
    final_val = value1/value2

  elif operator == "*":
    final_val = value1*value2

  print(final_val)

while (1):
  calculator ()
```

If you then perform arithmetic operations, it looks like this, for example:

```
Enter the 1st value: 5
Enter the 2nd value: 5
Enter the arithmetic operator: *
25
Enter the 1st value: 10
Enter the 2nd value: 15
Enter the arithmetic operator: +
25
Enter the 1st value: 10
Enter the 2nd value: 2
Enter the arithmetic operator: /
5.0
Enter the 1st value: 18
Enter the 2nd value: 7
Enter the arithmetic operator: -
11
Enter the 1st value: |
```

11.2 Project 2: Display of all prime numbers in an interval

In this project we want to write a script step by step that shows us all prime numbers in a certain range. That is, we want to be able to define, for example, the range 1 - 100 in the input and then output all prime numbers that exist in this range.

By the way, a prime number is a number that is divisible only by itself and 1 (without remainder), but is greater than 1.

Step 1: Definition of the area as user input

The range of values that the program is to check for prime numbers must be able to be specified as user input via the prompt. To do this, we define the upper and lower end of the range using two variables *lower* and *upper and* convert the input (strings) in turn to integers (int).

```
lower=int(input("Enter the lower limit: "))
upper=int(input("Enter the upper limit: "))
```

Step 2: Check for prime numbers

In this step, each number within the given range is to be checked to see if it is a prime number or not. For this purpose we use for, if and else statements.

```
for value in range (lower, upper):
    if value>1:
        for i in range (2, value):
            if(value%i)==0:
                break
        else:
            print(value,"\n")
```

In the instructions, *value* is the variable that is always incremented (incremented by 1) over the defined range between lower and upper value. At each step (iteration), the first conditional statement **if** first checks if the numeric value selected for the variable named *value* is greater than 1, since all prime numbers are greater than 1. The remaining statements are executed only if the numerical value selected for the variable named *value* is greater than 1 (nested statements). The next if statement at the next indented level then checks whether the selected value can be divided by any other values within the range without leaving any remainder. If there is any value that can divide the selected numeric value for the variable named *value* without having a remainder, the loop terminates and moves to the next iteration. On the other hand, if the conditional statement is **false**, the particular value of the variable *value is* output as a prime number in the prompt. This process continues until the entire specified range has been checked.

Step 3: Run the program continuously

Again, a mechanism should be implemented to keep the program running continuously, otherwise the program would only run for a single run and then stop. We implement this again with a simple while statement at the end of the code so that the program is executed continuously.

Below we see the complete Python script for the described project:

```
def check_primes():
    lower=int(input("Enter the lower limit: "))
    upper=int(input("Enter the upper limit: "))

    print("Prime numbers between ",lower, "and ",upper, "are: ")
    for value in range (lower, upper):
        if value>1:
            for i in range (2, value):
                if(value%i)==0:
                    break
            else:
                print(value,"\n")

while(1):
    check_primes()
```

A function named **check_primes()** has been defined, and all the statements described above have been placed inside the function so that the function in question can be executed continuously.

Here is the complete written code for a simple copy into the Python IDLE:

```
def check_primes():

  lower=int(input("Enter the lower limit: "))

  upper=int(input("Enter the upper limit: "))


  print("Prime numbers between ",lower, "and ",upper, "are: ")

  for value in range (lower,upper):

      if value>1:
```

```
    for i in range (2, value):
      if(value%i)==0:
        break
    else:
      print(value,"\n")
while(1):
  check_primes()
```

If you then perform the prime number check for specific ranges, it looks like this, for example:

```
Enter the lower limit: 5
Enter the upper limit: 25
Prime numbers between  5 and  25 are:
5

7

11

13

17

19

23

Enter the lower limit: 1
Enter the upper limit: 68
Prime numbers between  1 and  68 are:
```

11.3 Project 3: Calculator with graphical user interface (GUI)

This project illustrates step-by-step the development of a somewhat more complex calculator with an interactive graphical user interface (GUI) using the Tkinter module that we already learned about in the previous section. Similar to the first project, the calculator should also be able to perform basic arithmetic operations, but in addition it should give a clear idea of how to develop an interactive GUI application and look like this:

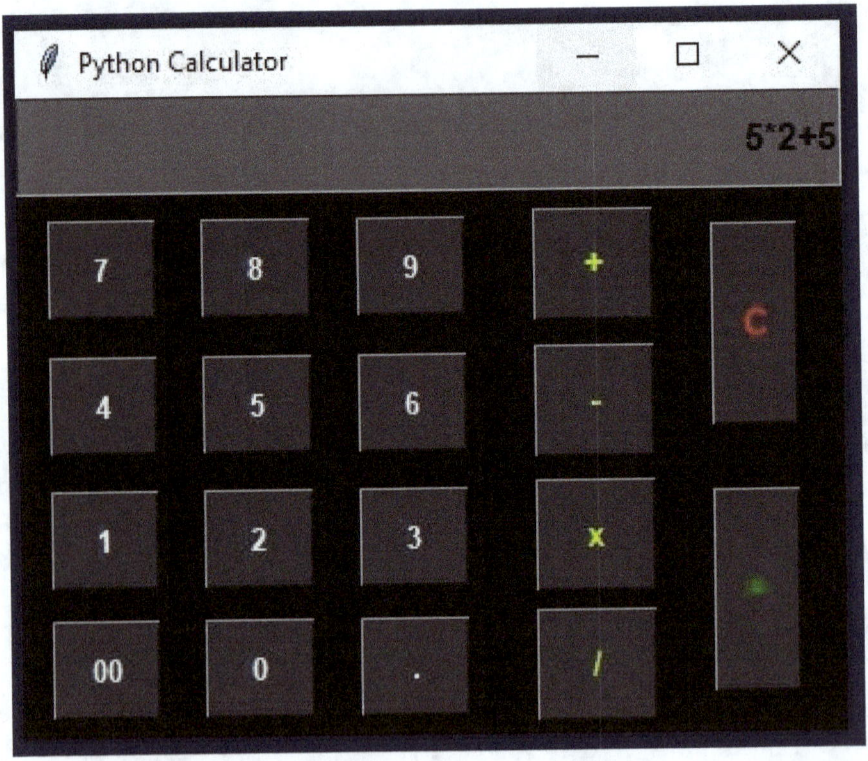

Step 1: Import the Tkinter package/ declare global variables

```
#Import tkinter library
from tkinter import *
```

```
# globally declare the expression variable
expression = ""
```

Step 2: Create GUI to display fields and buttons

```
if __name__ == "__main__":
    gui = Tk()
    gui.configure(background="gray5")
    gui.title("Python Calculator")
    gui.geometry("374x282")
    equation = StringVar()
```

Step 3: Setting up the GUI functionalities

In this step, using the Tkinter widgets, we define what happens when a user clicks a button on the calculator.

When one clicks on one of the buttons, the **enter()** method should be called. This method passes numbers or arithmetic operators depending on which button was clicked. Once the value is passed, the numbers or operators are stored in the expression variable. Before storing the value or the activator of the expression variable, we still need to convert it to a string using the **str()** method.

```
#Function that updates the expression
def Enter(number):
    global expression

    # Concatenation of string
    expression = expression + str(number)

    #Update the expression using the set method
    equation.set(expression)
```

The = button calculates the total string stored in the expression variable. The **eval()** function helps to perform the arithmetic operations of the variable and returns the total value.

```
#Function to evaluate the final output
def pressequal():
    try:
        global expression

        #eval function to evaluate the expression
        total = str(eval(expression))
        equation.set(total)

        #initialize the expression variable by empty string
        expression = ""

    #If an error occurs this except block will handle it
    except:
        equation.set(" error ")
        expression = ""
```

The "**C**" button of our calculator clears the contents of the display, i.e. the previously entered values. So when we click on the "C" (clear) button of our calculator, we want the **clear()** method to be called. The variable *expression* is created as an empty string.

```
#this function is used to clear the display field
def clear():
    global expression
    expression = ""
    equation.set("")
```

Python provides a wide range of widgets that help in developing user-friendly GUIs. In this project we will use the buttons and text fields we have already learned about.

```
#create a Display field inside the window
Display_field = Entry(gui, font=('arial', 12, 'bold'), bg='dimgray',
                      textvariable=equation, justify= RIGHT)

Display_field.grid(columnspan=6, ipadx=95, row=0, column=0, ipady = 10)
```

```
#create buttons and place them at a specific place
button7 = Button(gui, text=' 7 ', fg='white', bg='gray28',
                 command=lambda: Enter(7), height=2, width=5,
                 font=('arial', 10, 'bold'))
button7.grid(row=2, column=0,  padx=10, pady=10)


button8 = Button(gui, text=' 8 ', fg='white', bg='gray28',
                 command=lambda: Enter(8), height=2, width=5,
                  font=('arial', 10, 'bold'))
button8.grid(row=2, column=1)


button9 = Button(gui, text=' 9 ', fg='white', bg='gray28',
                 command=lambda: Enter(9), height=2, width=5,
                  font=('arial', 10, 'bold'))
button9.grid(row=2, column=2)


button4 = Button(gui, text=' 4 ', fg='white', bg='gray28',
                 command=lambda: Enter(4), height=2, width=5,
                 font=('arial', 10, 'bold'))
button4.grid(row=3, column=0)


button5 = Button(gui, text=' 5 ', fg='white', bg='gray28',
                 command=lambda: Enter(5), height=2, width=5,
                 font=('arial', 10, 'bold'))
```

The **mainloop()** method runs the calculator window in an infinite loop. The pocket calculator is executed until the user closes the window manually.

```
#run the application
gui.mainloop()
```

Below is the complete code in image form (the text form for easy copying will also follow):

File Edit Format Run Options Window Help

```
#import tkinter library
from tkinter import *

# globally declare the expression variable
expression = ""

#Function that updates the expression
def Enter(number):
    global expression

    # concatenation of string
    expression = expression + str(number)

    #update the expression using the set method
    equation.set(expression)

#Function to evaluate the final output
def pressequal():
    try:
        global expression

        #eval function to evaluate the expression
        total = str(eval(expression))
        equation.set(total)

        #initialize the expression variable by empty string
        expression = ""

    #if an error occurs then except block will handle it
    except:
        equation.set(" error ")
        expression = ""
```

```
def clear():
    global expression
    expression = ""
    equation.set("")

if __name__ == "__main__":

    gui = Tk()

    gui.configure(background="gray5")

    gui.title("Python Calculator")

    gui.geometry("374x282")

    equation = StringVar()

    Display_field = Entry(gui, font=('arial', 12, 'bold'), bg='dimgray',
                          textvariable=equation, justify= RIGHT)

    Display_field.grid(columnspan=6, ipadx=95, row=0, column=0, ipady = 10)

    button7 = Button(gui, text=' 7 ', fg='white', bg='gray28',
                     command=lambda: Enter(7), height=2, width=5,
                     font=('arial', 10, 'bold'))
    button7.grid(row=2, column=0,  padx=10, pady=10)
```

```
#create buttons and place them at a specific place
button7 = Button(gui, text=' 7 ', fg='white', bg='gray28',
                 command=lambda: Enter(7), height=2, width=5,
                 font=('arial', 10, 'bold'))
button7.grid(row=2, column=0,  padx=10, pady=10)


button8 = Button(gui, text=' 8 ', fg='white', bg='gray28',
                 command=lambda: Enter(8), height=2, width=5,
                  font=('arial', 10, 'bold'))
button8.grid(row=2, column=1)


button9 = Button(gui, text=' 9 ', fg='white', bg='gray28',
                 command=lambda: Enter(9), height=2, width=5,
                  font=('arial', 10, 'bold'))
button9.grid(row=2, column=2)


button4 = Button(gui, text=' 4 ', fg='white', bg='gray28',
                 command=lambda: Enter(4), height=2, width=5,
                 font=('arial', 10, 'bold'))
button4.grid(row=3, column=0)


button5 = Button(gui, text=' 5 ', fg='white', bg='gray28',
                 command=lambda: Enter(5), height=2, width=5,
                 font=('arial', 10, 'bold'))
button5.grid(row=3, column=1)


button6 = Button(gui, text=' 6 ', fg='white', bg='gray28',
                 command=lambda: Enter(6), height=2, width=5,
```

```
button1 = Button(gui, text=' 1 ', fg='white', bg='gray28',
                command=lambda: Enter(1), height=2, width=5,
                font=('arial', 10, 'bold'))
button1.grid(row=4, column=0)


button2 = Button(gui, text=' 2 ', fg='white', bg='gray28',
                command=lambda: Enter(2), height=2, width=5,
                font=('arial', 10, 'bold'))
button2.grid(row=4, column=1)


button3 = Button(gui, text=' 3 ', fg='white', bg='gray28',
                command=lambda: Enter(3), height=2, width=5,
                font=('arial', 10, 'bold'))
button3.grid(row=4, column=2, padx=10, pady=10)


button0 = Button(gui, text=' 0 ', fg='white', bg='gray28',
                command=lambda: Enter(0), height=2, width=5,
                font=('arial', 10, 'bold'))
button0.grid(row=5, column=1)


buttonPara = Button(gui, text=' 00 ', fg='white', bg='gray28',
                command=lambda: Enter('00'), height=2, width=5,
                font=('arial', 10, 'bold'))
buttonPara.grid(row=5, column=0)
```

```
buttonDecimal = Button(gui, text=' . ', fg='white', bg='gray28',
                    command=lambda: Enter('.'), height=2, width=5,
                    font=('arial', 10, 'bold'))
buttonDecimal.grid(row=5, column=2)


Addition_btn = Button(gui, text=' + ', fg='olivedrab2', bg='gray28',
             command=lambda: Enter("+"), height=2, width=5,
             font=('arial', 11, 'bold'))
Addition_btn.grid(row=2, column=4)


Subtraction_btn = Button(gui, text=' - ', fg='olivedrab2', bg='gray28',
             command=lambda: Enter("-"), height=2, width=5,
             font=('arial', 11, 'bold'))
Subtraction_btn.grid(row=3, column=4)


Multiplication_Btn = Button(gui, text=' x ', fg='olivedrab2', bg='gray28',
             command=lambda: Enter("*"), height=2, width=5,
             font=('arial', 11, 'bold'))
Multiplication_Btn.grid(row=4, column=4)


Division_Btn = Button(gui, text=' / ', fg='olivedrab2', bg='gray28',
             command=lambda: Enter("/"), height=2, width=5,
             font=('arial', 11, 'bold'))
Division_Btn.grid(row=5, column=4)
```

```
clear_Btn = Button(gui, text='C', fg='firebrick2', bg='gray28',
           command=clear, height=4, width=3,
           font=('arial', 12, 'bold'))
clear_Btn.grid(row=2, rowspan=2, column=5, padx=15, pady=15)


Equal_Btn = Button(gui, text='=', fg='Green4', bg='gray28',
           command=pressequal, height=4, width=3,
           font=('arial', 12, 'bold'))
Equal_Btn .grid(row=4, rowspan=2, column=5)

Run the application
gui.mainloop()
```

Our finished calculator with a graphical user interface will look like this:

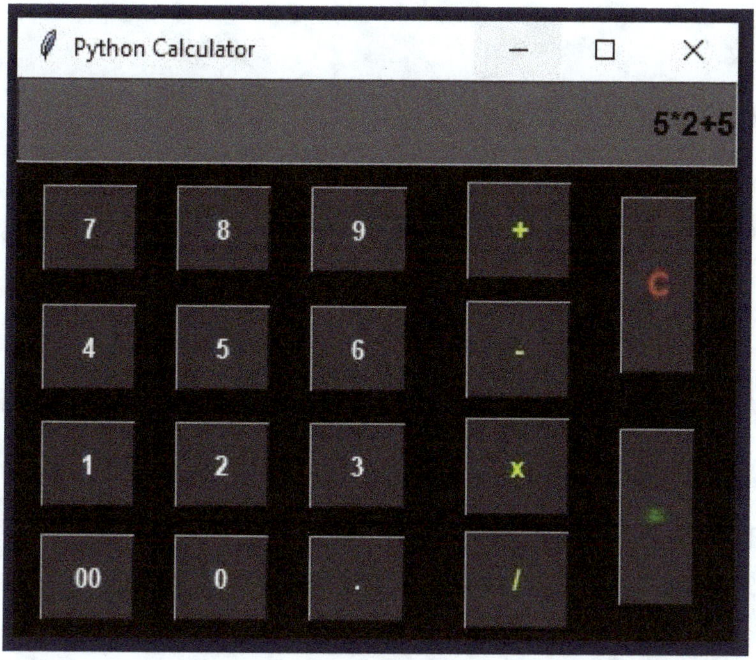

Here is the complete written code for a simple copy into the Python IDLE:

```
#Import tkinter library
from tkinter import *

# globally declare the expression variable
expression = ""

#Function that updates the expression
def Enter(number):
    global expression

    # concatenation of string
    expression = expression + str(number)
```

```
    #Update the expression using the SET method
    equation.set(expression)

#Function to evaluate the final output
def pressequal():
    try:
        global expression

        #eval function to evaluate the expression
        total = str(eval(expression))
        equation.set(total)

        #initialize the expression variable by empty string
        expression = ""

    #If an error occurs this except block will handle it
    except:
        equation.set(" error ")
        expression = ""

#This function is used to clear the Display field
def clear():
    global expression
    expression = ""
    equation.set("")

if __name__ == "__main__":
```

```
gui = Tk() #Creating a basic window
gui.configure(background="gray5") #color for the window
gui.title("Python Calculator") #title of the window
gui.geometry("374x282") #Size for the created window

equation = StringVar() #create an instance using stringVar variable class

#create a Display field inside the window
Display_field = Entry(gui, font=('arial', 12, 'bold'), bg='dimgray',
                textvariable=equation, justify= RIGHT)

Display_field.grid(columnspan=6, ipadx=95, row=0, column=0, ipady = 10)

#create buttons and place them at a specific place
button7 = Button(gui, text=' 7 ', fg='white', bg='gray28',
          command=lambda: Enter(7), height=2, width=5,
          font=('arial', 10, 'bold'))
button7.grid(row=2, column=0,  padx=10, pady=10)

button8 = Button(gui, text=' 8 ', fg='white', bg='gray28',
          command=lambda: Enter(8), height=2, width=5,
          font=('arial', 10, 'bold'))
button8.grid(row=2, column=1)

button9 = Button(gui, text=' 9 ', fg='white', bg='gray28',
          command=lambda: Enter(9), height=2, width=5,
          font=('arial', 10, 'bold'))
button9.grid(row=2, column=2)
```

```
button4 = Button(gui, text=' 4 ', fg='white', bg='gray28',
          command=lambda: Enter(4), height=2, width=5,
          font=('arial', 10, 'bold'))
button4.grid(row=3, column=0)

button5 = Button(gui, text=' 5 ', fg='white', bg='gray28',
          command=lambda: Enter(5), height=2, width=5,
          font=('arial', 10, 'bold'))
button5.grid(row=3, column=1)

button6 = Button(gui, text=' 6 ', fg='white', bg='gray28',
          command=lambda: Enter(6), height=2, width=5,
          font=('arial', 10, 'bold'))
button6.grid(row=3, column=2)


button1 = Button(gui, text=' 1 ', fg='white', bg='gray28',
          command=lambda: Enter(1), height=2, width=5,
          font=('arial', 10, 'bold'))
button1.grid(row=4, column=0)

button2 = Button(gui, text=' 2 ', fg='white', bg='gray28',
          command=lambda: Enter(2), height=2, width=5,
          font=('arial', 10, 'bold'))
button2.grid(row=4, column=1)

button3 = Button(gui, text=' 3 ', fg='white', bg='gray28',
          command=lambda: Enter(3), height=2, width=5,
```

```
            font=('arial', 10, 'bold'))
button3.grid(row=4, column=2, padx=10, pady=10)

buttonO = Button(gui, text=' 0 ', fg='white', bg='gray28',
            command=lambda: Enter(0), height=2, width=5,
            font=('arial', 10, 'bold'))
buttonO.grid(row=5, column=1)

buttonPara = Button(gui, text=' 00 ', fg='white', bg='gray28',
            command=lambda: Enter('00'), height=2, width=5,
            font=('arial', 10, 'bold'))
buttonPara.grid(row=5, column=0)

buttonDecimal = Button(gui, text=' . ', fg='white', bg='gray28',
            command=lambda: Enter('.'), height=2, width=5,
            font=('arial', 10, 'bold'))
buttonDecimal.grid(row=5, column=2)

Addition_btn = Button(gui, text=' + ', fg='olivedrab2', bg='gray28',
        command=lambda: Enter("+"), height=2, width=5,
        font=('arial', 11, 'bold'))
Addition_btn.grid(row=2, column=4)

Subtraction_btn = Button(gui, text=' - ', fg='olivedrab2', bg='gray28',
        command=lambda: Enter("-"), height=2, width=5,
        font=('arial', 11, 'bold'))
Subtraction_btn.grid(row=3, column=4)

Multiplication_Btn = Button(gui, text=' x ', fg='olivedrab2', bg='gray28',
```

```
        command=lambda: Enter("*"), height=2, width=5,
        font=('arial', 11, 'bold'))
    Multiplication_Btn.grid(row=4, column=4)


    Division_Btn = Button(gui, text=' / ', fg='olivedrab2', bg='gray28',
        command=lambda: Enter("/"), height=2, width=5,
        font=('arial', 11, 'bold'))
    Division_Btn.grid(row=5, column=4)


    clear_Btn = Button(gui, text='C', fg='firebrick2', bg='gray28',
        command=clear, height=4, width=3,
        font=('arial', 12, 'bold'))
    clear_Btn.grid(row=2, rowspan=2, column=5, padx=15, pady=15)


    Equal_Btn = Button(gui, text='=', fg='Green4', bg='gray28',
        command=pressequal, height=4, width=3,
        font=('arial', 12, 'bold'))
    Equal_Btn .grid(row=4, rowspan=2, column=5)

#run the application
gui.mainloop()
```

12 Troubleshooting - common beginner mistakes

In general, programming in Python is not very difficult if you follow certain basic rules that have been taught in this course. However, if something does not work, this short lesson should help. Alternatively, you can look for troubleshooting guides online or visit a forum and ask experienced users for advice.

Conflicts between Python versions

It is important to know that sometimes there are several major versions of Python at the same time: currently, for example, Python 2 and Python 3. It may happen that the same script does not work in a different Python version - than the version in which it was developed - because there are small differences from version to version. Therefore, it is advisable to pay attention to the version of the Python environment in case a script that worked fine before suddenly gives error messages.

Syntax errors: indents, tabs and spaces

Indentations are very important in the Python programming language because the language itself requires very precise indentation levels. Otherwise, errors will be generated. On the other hand, incorrect indentations are more serious in cases where no errors are generated, but the functionality of the script differs from the expected result. It is recommended to use four spaces as one indentation, but not tab characters. Also, be sure to use the correct number and correct usage of syntax elements such as ":" or "(" or ")".

Error in variable names

As a programmer, one should be very careful when using variable names, since a single difference in a variable name or even a typo during the compilation or execution phase will result in an error or bug. More importantly, Python is a case-sensitive programming language, so care must be taken to use upper and lower case letters correctly. Also, you should use variable names sensibly. That is, when you yourself look at the program script at a later time, or when another programmer looks at it, the variable name itself, should already hint at or somewhat anticipate the meaning or intended use of that variable. In this way, you can greatly facilitate the comprehensibility of the script or even a debugging process.

Closing words

Excellent!

You've done it, you've worked through the beginner course. Congratulations!

In this book I have tried to bring you the basic knowledge for programming in Python simply explained closer. I hope that I have succeeded to some extent and that this book has brought you a well understandable and practical introduction to the world of programming and in particular to the world of Python and that you are now eager to find out what you could program!

The goal of this book was to introduce you to what the basic principles in programming (with Python) are. It should be a book that both creates an understanding of the theoretical background knowledge and trains practical application skills.

With this basic course you should now know everything you need as a beginner for the first programming in Python! Of course, it makes sense not to stop at this point and rather look into an advanced book to learn even more about Python or even other programming languages.

Together we have accomplished quite a bit in this course! Be justifiably proud of yourself if you made it to the end! **If you enjoyed this book, I would be very happy if you leave me a rating and a short feedback, as well as recommend the book! Thank you very much.**

One final tip:
If you ever get stuck, take a look at the following websites, where you can find lots and great materials as well as the community on Python: www.python.org/doc and www.phyton.org/community respectively.

If you are also interested in other books of mine on similar topics, be sure to take another look at the next pages.

Thank you very much!

Books on topics you might also like

All books are available online on the usual sales platforms. It's best to just search for the title, or feel free to visit my author page. Some of the books may not be published yet and will be released or found soon. Take a look at the books of your choice and your copy as e-book or paperback!

3D Printing:

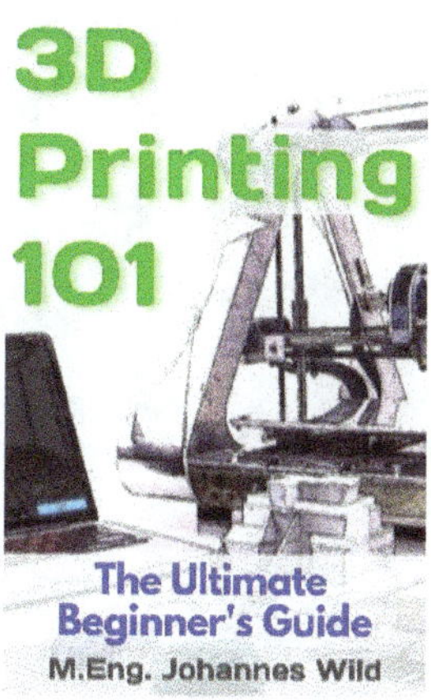

CAD, FEM, CAM (3D Object Creation, Design, Simulation):

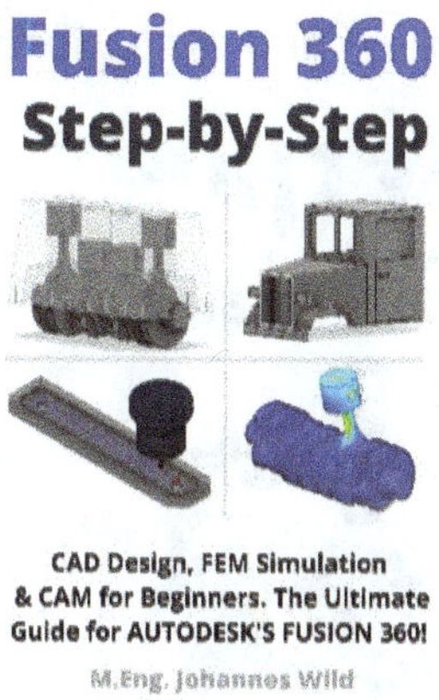

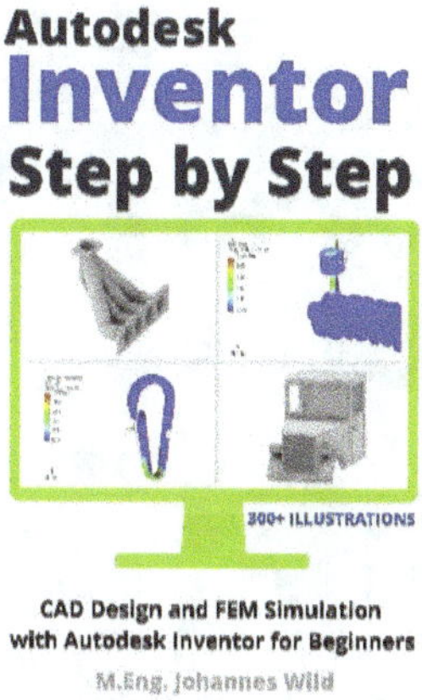

Electrical Engineering:

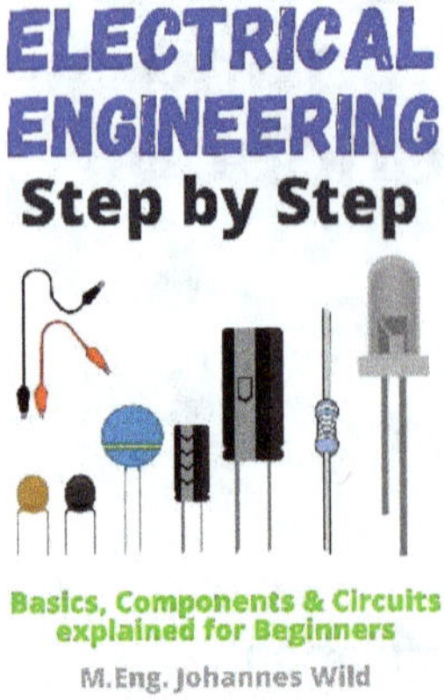

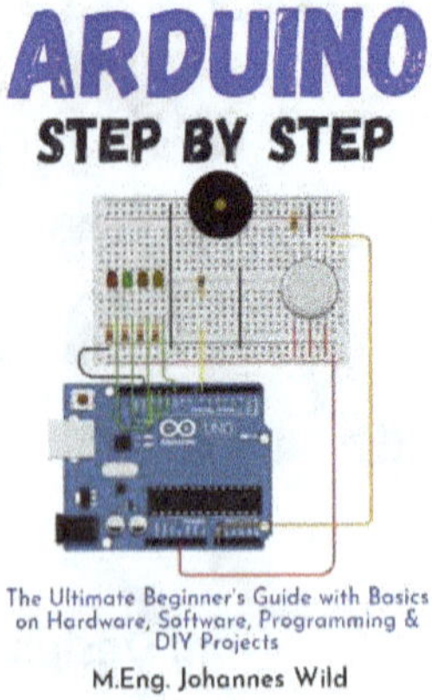

Programming and other Software:

There are also identical video courses for some of these books:

Fusion 360 Step by Step | CAD, FEM & CAM for Beginners
The Ultimate Hands-On Guide for AUTODESK FUSION 360! Learn Design, Simulation, Manufacturing and more from an engineer!
M.Eng. Johannes Wild
4.7 ★★★★★ (10)
3.5 total hours • 24 lectures • Beginner
Highest rated

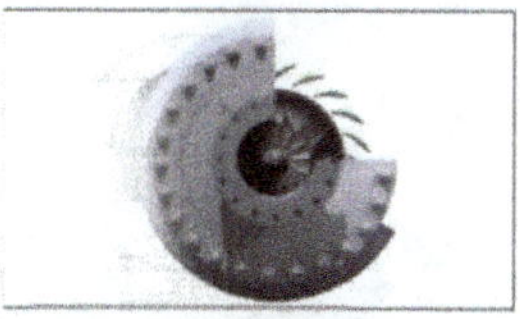

CAD Design 101 | 3D modelling for beginners (by an engineer)
The ultimate beginner's guide on how to create 3D objects with free CAD software for 3D printing and much more!
M.Eng. Johannes Wild
4.4 ★★★★★ (10)
1.5 total hours • 15 lectures • All Levels

3D Printing 101 | The Ultimate Beginner's Guide
A Hard- & Software All-in-One created by an engineer. Designed for an instant start into the world of 3D printing!
M.Eng. Johannes Wild
4.2 ★★★★☆ (17)
1.5 total hours • 20 lectures • All Levels

Fusion 360 | CAD Design Projects – Part 1
10 simple to intermediate CAD design projects for intermediate to advanced users (explained step by step)
M.Eng. Johannes Wild
2 total hours • 12 lectures • Intermediate
New

...

For purchase you can search for my name at www.udemy.com :

M.Eng. Johannes Wild, or use the following link:

www.udemy.com/courses/search/?src=ukw&q=m.eng.+johannes+wild

Enroll today and deepen your knowledge!

Imprint of the author / publisher

Johannes Wild
c/o RA Matutis
Berliner Straße 57
14467 Potsdam
Germany

Phone: +49 15257887206
Email: 3dtech@gmx.de
Internet: www.3dtech-3dprinting.com

This work is protected by copyright

Thank you so much for choosing this book!

www.ingramcontent.com/pod-product-compliance
Lightning Source LLC
LaVergne TN
LVHW012335060326
832902LV00012B/1904